A Shor

of INDIAN
RAILWAYS

A Short History
of INDIAN
RAILWAYS

RAJENDRA B. AKLEKAR

RUPA

Published by
Rupa Publications India Pvt. Ltd 2019
7/16, Ansari Road, Daryaganj
New Delhi 110002

Sales centres:
Allahabad Bengaluru Chennai
Hyderabad Jaipur Kathmandu
Kolkata Mumbai

ISBN: 978-93-5333-287-7

Fifth impression 2022

10 9 8 7 6 5

The moral right of the author has been asserted.

Printed in India

Contents

Foreword   vii

Introduction   xi

1. The First Experiments   1
2. Ancestors of Indian Railways   10
3. Railways Begin Their Operations   26
4. The Arrival of the Railways   46
5. Rail Web Spreads   54
6. The Indian Mutiny and the Railways   71
7. Rail Gauge and Ghosts   83
8. New Century, New Life   102
9. The Animated Rail Life   114
10. Crime and Romance   127
11. Notes from World War II   141
12. Freedom Struggle and Partition   150
13. Rail Tales from Independent India   165

14. Trains of Progress and Politics   177
15. Of Metros and High Speed Rail   187

Conclusion   209
Acknowledgements   211
Index   213

Foreword

When I first started out as a broadcaster, I was told, 'Always remember you have to tell a story.' I have kept that adage in mind. Ever since I was a child, I have been a devotee of the railways. It has been almost eighty years now since my earliest encounters with the Indian Railways, travelling to Darjeeling where I went to school, or to Puri for the winter holidays. So I have always sought opportunities to tell railway tales in my broadcasts, films and books.

In the TV film *From Karachi to the Khyber*, I have told the story of workers lowered from cliff tops on platforms having to find their own footholds so that they could blast a route with explosives through the mountainous Bolan Pass to take the railway to the Pakistani city of Quetta. In the same film, there is the story of an engineer who persuaded hostile Pathan tribesmen to allow him to build the line through the Khyber Pass by telling them the trains would go so slowly they could easily be looted. In another film, *An Indian Summer of Steam*, there is a maharaja who remembered having his own royal train, and a steam engine driver who burst into tears when his engine broke down.

I have told tales, too, of my encounters with passengers. There was the passenger on the Khyber Mail who I found reading my book *No Full Stops in India*. He told me I had no reason to be pleased about this, because he was reading a pirated copy, and went on to say, 'Now write *No Punctuation Marks in Pakistan*.' Another time, while making a radio programme about the Mumbai–Howrah Mail running on the Raj's Imperial Mail route via Allahabad, I asked a passenger whether I could interview her. She replied, 'By all means, but you should really interview my husband. He is a comedian who specializes in imitating the different ways passengers snore on trains.' That would have been wonderful material for my programme, but unfortunately, the husband had just got off the train.

There have been my encounters with the railway staff too. A favourite story, which I have told more than once, concerns my suggesting to a travelling ticket examiner that it was a bit hard having to pay a superfast surcharge to crawl up the steep climb from Chandigarh to Kalka. The outraged official replied, 'This *is* a superfast train. It is only going slow.'

On another occasion, when I enquired why my train had stopped, I was told, 'line punctured', which, I discovered, meant there was a cracked rail.

The poet Robert Browning wrote of 'the story always old and always new'. I have found stories so effective in journalism because, although they tell of the past, they never lose their freshness. They instruct; for instance, the construction of the line through the Bolan Pass illustrates the ingenuity of Victorian engineers, while the anecdote of the Pathan tribesmen provides a telling example of the opposition the railway builders faced. Stories like my encounters with passengers and railway staff entertain, and so, are an important element in keeping listeners', viewers' and readers' attention.

As historian Rajendra B. Aklekar is a storyteller too, and a railway devotee, he has chosen to tell stories, or tales, to narrate the history of Indian Railways from the 1830s to today. His stories instruct and entertain, bringing the past of the Indian Railways alive in the present. They will entertain as well as instruct, thereby encouraging Indians to be proud of their railways' past and to ensure that those railways play a crucial role in the future.

Mark Tully

Introduction

When the first railway lines and steam-puffing locomotives were seen moving on this land, it caused a stir in what was a traditional and culturally-rich society. It led to surprise, fear, superstition, gossip and awe. With the fascination for speed and locomotion, acceptance for this 'new' technology came in slowly, with caution, but eventually, completely. And amidst this clash of cultures sprung fascinating tales of people, the changing social life of the country's remote villages and the people's journeys. This book is about those tales—tales that made Indian Railways what it is today, tales that look at its legacy, growth and development.

This work, a compilation of anecdotes and sketches of the Indian Railways, was first suggested to me by Rupa Publications' CEO, Shri Kapish Mehra. It took more time than expected to bring it to fruition. It involved collating the right anecdotes from numerous sources, building research around them and ground work—from visiting India's oldest functional station at Chennai to tracking down one of the key team members behind the subcontinent's first superfast train, the Rajdhani Express—

and then documenting all of them chronologically. There were numerous ups and downs throughout the process, and at the end of it, I started building a narrative to weave the stories together, thanks to the persistent editor Shri Rudra Sharma who kept suggesting improvizations to the draft to mould it into what has now turned out to be, hopefully, a fabulous book.

The research was not without its own set of challenges. While in some cases there was a multiplicity of sources, some anecdotes were closer to fiction, a few had authentication problems and others had vague narratives and unclear data. Narrowing down from among these to select a few great tales from such huge volumes of data to capture the flavour of almost two centuries was an interesting journey altogether.

While every decade had its own adventure, the World Wars and the Partition were the worst moments for the Indian Railways, as infrastructure was stripped to suit the times. In independent India, success stories like the construction of the 760–km stretch of the western coast rail line, the Konkan Railway, through one of the most difficult terrains of the country, described by British TV presenter Chris Tarrant as India's Extreme Railway, added a contemporary positive flavour to it all.

I felt adding an episode on one of the most gruesome incidents in the twenty-first century—the serial train bomb blasts of Mumbai in 2006—which I personally witnessed and covered for a national newspaper, was necessary to include in an effort to make people aware of modern-day security threats to the railways.

Research for this book has been a learning process and has widened my horizons, offering me kaleidoscopic perspectives to look at the same old Indian Railways in many different ways and forms.

Rajendra B. Aklekar
Mumbai, March 2019

1

THE FIRST EXPERIMENTS
Looking at Physical Links

EXPLORATIONS

The old-era rails that supported the roof of the only older-looking platform at this railway station, about five kilometres from Chennai Central station, had revealed nothing to me. The markings did not make any sense. They seemed gibberish. If the rails had been constructed in 1956, it was probably too late to find any link to the origins of the station that was well over a hundred years old. The other platforms around it were either newer or being rebuilt.

I was standing at India's oldest functional railway station—Royapuram—in Chennai, south India, in 2017. Opened to the public on 28 June 1856, Royapuram station was inaugurated by the then governor of Madras, Lord Harris, as part of the newly formed Madras Railway. The first train of south India, manufactured by

Simpson & Co. Ltd., started its journey from Royapuram to Walajah Road with 300 people, three days after the inauguration—on 1 July 1856. The station remained the headquarters of the Madras and Southern Mahratta Railway until 1922, when it was shifted to Chennai Egmore.

I thought I had a chance of finding significant markers or something of historical significance on the platform I was at, closer to the station's main building. This was the one building that was present in the oldest photographs of the station and had witnessed its growth, or rather, its decline. I was fixated on the relics here, including the station's signboard, which had the word 'Royapuram' painted over the once-etched 'Rayapuram', the station's old name.

The markings and the type of rails that form the support of a station's roof and its pillars, base and brackets overhead usually give an important lead on the station's and the line's genesis. For example, the year and the name of the foundry or the railway company the rails originally belonged to give us insight into the history of the station and the line in general.

But the rail markings here on this platform simply said 'XII/1956 ←' and the rails were modern and flat-footed, unlike the ones used in the earlier days of the Indian Railways.[1] So these were newer, with little link to the station's origins.

I still had to look around. The tall Gothic and fluted columns, now painted over, the foyer, the arched doorways

---

[1] India's earliest railway companies used 'double-headed' or 'bull-headed' rails as per the prevalent technology in those days.

and entrances, the wood-beamed high roof and decorative metal brackets were the only significant relics visible at Royapuram station. The station's building, rather what remained of the old building—renovated a decade ago, circa 2005—was a shadow of its former self. It appeared majestic even in its current form. It seemed as if it was looking down upon the electric trains passing by. After all, it belonged to a different age—the glorious era that had gone by, when railways were the future and trains the fastest mode of communication.

Historically and officially, the 1853 Bombay-Thana railway line (now Mumbai-Thane) was the oldest passenger railway line in the country, but none of the stations on this route exist in their original form. Royapuram does, though I don't know how long it will continue to do so, with the Southern Railway now planning an expansion of the station. This essentially means an upgrade—more lines, more trains and more passenger amenities.

This is why I had come here—just to be at the station and spend a few hours trying to connect with it. And I must say, it still is in a class of its own, standing out among all the stations in Chennai.

IN SEARCH OF MARKERS

A few kilometres away, after switching local trains or EMUs (electric multiple units), I reached Chennai Egmore—another landmark. Egmore is the anglicized form of 'Ezhumbur', the name of a pre-British-era village situated on the northern banks of the Coovum river. The station is the arrival and departure point for trains connecting southern and central Tamil Nadu and Kerala. With Mughal-style architecture, including semicircular domes and carvings, the spacious station resembles a palace. Built between 1905 and 1908 with fine granite stones, ornamental brackets, dripstones and friezes, this station is a strong link to the history and origin of the railways in India. It even has a few iron pillars embossed with the words 'Made in Porto Novo', Porto Novo being one of India's oldest ironworks plants.

It is interesting to note that Porto Novo, or Parangipettai, located on the north bank of the Vellar river, on the Coromandel coast, has a lot more than its iron and steel history to boast about. It is about 30 km from Cuddalore district in Tamil Nadu. Porto Novo was not only ground zero for the first iron and steel industry plant in India in the 1830s, but also possibly the starting point for the country's steam railways.[2] The small plant of Porto Novo Iron Company[3] on the Madras coast, started by Josiah Marshall Heath in 1830, produced pig iron at the rate of 40 tonnes a week.[4] This was the first notable

---

[2]J.T. Smith, 'Notes of some experiments made by Captain A. Cotton, upon Mr Avery's steam engine,' *Reports, Correspondence and Original Papers on Various Professional Subjects Connected with the Duties of the Corps of Engineers of Madras Presidency, vol.1.* chap.11, (Madras, 1839): 95

[3]D. Sim, 'Report upon the Coleroon Annicuts,' Ibid, chap.7, p.142

[4]'Zerah Colbur, Indian Iron and Steel Company—1,' *Engineering—An Illustrated Weekly Journal* (April 1867): 307

effort of this magnitude in India. Traces of this iconic firm are imprinted on the pillars of Chennai Egmore station. I was standing there looking for these historical markers.

Walking up and down the station for hours amidst a clutter of passengers rushing with their luggage, continuous announcements in three languages about train arrivals and departures, my eyes were fixed on those pillars. After much strain, I did spot faint markings, but they were illegible, thickly painted over and almost disappearing.

The two sets of twenty-plus tall iron pillars supporting the platform's main arched roof were made of cast iron. There were markings on two of the old pillars—to be precise, on the sixth and the eleventh ones—on one of the platforms. But they were too high up, faint and buried under numerous layers of thick paint, and entangled wires of the station's Wi-Fi routers. I counted the pillars again, made mental notes, and decided to leave after four hours. After all, I had to return to Mumbai.

EMPTY-HANDED, BUT NOT COMPLETELY SO

Even though the physical links to India's rail history are being wiped out slowly as generations pass, the stories of how these lines got built and are still functioning perfectly today are fascinating. Porto Novo was one of the key beginnings for modern travel in the country. Rummaging through the archives of the Indian Railways and libraries and places like railway societies and heritage rail clubs, of which I have been a long-time member, I chanced upon a few documents and books—a few in the public domain and a few rare ones in the history of the Indian Railways—and this is what I found.

The story of Porto Novo is the story of the railways and steam engines in India—the story of India's first railway plans and the running of the first trains. The next few pages will run you through the historical journey of how the foundations of the railways were slowly getting laid—year-wise, sequentially, and how they spread across the continent.

The trains were coming!

THE FIRSTS—BOMBAY (1823) AND CALCUTTA (1828)

An engine is not always a locomotive or a railway engine. It is a motor or a machine that converts one form of energy into mechanical energy. In my previous book, *Halt Station India: The Dramatic Tale of the Nation's First Lines*, I quoted the very first documented references that I could find at the time of the use of steam engines in India. They pointed to Bombay (now Mumbai) in 1823 and Calcutta (now Kolkata) in 1828. Of course, these were stationary engines, used for limited purposes. While the ones in Bombay were used for a cannonball-making factory and to drive a water mill, the one in Calcutta was a nineteenth-century 'Make in India' version, made by an Indian blacksmith from Titigur—Goluk Chandra—who won a prize of ₹50 for its manufacture.

Remember, the world's first public railway—between Stockton and Darlington, England—opened in 1825. Well, the engines in Bombay had come into existence before that iconic world event in England. Reports say that as early as 1823, the Gun Carriage Factory in Colaba, then Bombay, manufacturing cannonballs and wheels, had several machines running on steam at a frantic pace. A year later, in 1824, when the world's first public railway was yet to be opened, Bombay saw another large stationary steam engine (one used for driving mills and factories) launched for public use, with cattle-driven Persian wheels pumping out water from wells to tanks. Inaugurated on 17 May 1824, this apparatus was built by the Parsi merchant and philanthropist Seth Framji Cowasji Banaji[5] to tide over the water crisis in Bombay.[6]

---

[5]Khoshru Navrosji Banaji, *Memoirs of the Late Framji Cowasji Banaji* (Bombay Gazette Steam Printing Press, 1892), chap.5, pp.28–32

[6]"Kalpana Desai, 'The Role of Parsis in the Urbanization of Mumbai in the Nineteenth Century,' Nawaz Modi, ed., *The Parsis in Western India: 1818 to 1920,* (Allied Publishers, Nov. 1998) Part 2, chap.8, p.156

Note: Circa 1814, the Bombay government decided to develop a new area at Kamatipura to meet the need for habitable space for the growing population. As the area faced acute shortage of water, two large water reservoirs were dug up and connected to the larger water tank in the area that had been built by Seth Cowasji Patel in 1780s at Khetwadi in Girgaum and named after him as Cawasji Patel tank (CP tank). But the arrangement of pipes worked only when the CP tank was full, leading to a crisis. It was another Parsi seth Framji Cawasji Banaji who saved the situation by sinking three wells and pumping water from these wells to the tanks by a Persian wheel run by bullocks and a steam engine. It was inaugurated on 17 May 1824. Centuries later, the areas, now beyond recognition, are still called Do Tanki and CP Tank.

Four years later, on the eastern coast in Calcutta, Goluk Chandra built and demonstrated, without any Englishman's help, a stationary steam engine, and won a prize at the Agri Horticultural Society's meeting.

It seems Chandra had been closely observing the working of missionary William Carey's 12 horsepower steam engine, which was brought from England to run a paper mill. Manufactured by Thwaites, Hick and Rothwell, who were engineers from Bolton, Lancashire, Carey's machine is known to be the first steam engine imported to India. And Goluk Chandra, after studying it, built his own!

It is important to remember that we are talking about the 1820s—a time with no communication, and only primitive transportation methods. In such a scenario, local inventions usually remained local and were quickly forgotten.

THE PORTO NOVO STORY

Let's go back to Porto Novo. It has been documented that in the 1830s, rotary steam engines, patented by William Avery of Syracuse, New York, were used for construction of canals. Avery's steam engine was basically an updated aeolipile, a Heron's engine—a form of steam engine that has been in existence since at least the first century BCE and named after Hero of Alexandria, who came up with the first description of the engine.[7]

---

[7]'India's First Railways,' Dec 2011, IRFCA, http://www.irfca.org/docs/history/india-first-railways.html

These rotary steam engines—widely mentioned as the 'new mechanical agent' or 'machine'—had made their way to the Madras Corps of Engineers and were being experimented with for various uses, including working on railroads as locomotives by General Sir Arthur Thomas Cotton[8] of the Madras Engineers KCSI[9].

While the stationary steam engines were used to power a lathe, the conclusions deduced from the experiments on these 'mechanical agents' eventually led to the 'construction' of what is documented as the first running steam locomotive in India—at Red Hills near Madras in 1838.

[8]General Sir Arthur Thomas Cotton of the Madras Engineers KCSI (15 May 1803–24 July 1899) is the English stalwart known to have devoted his life to the construction of irrigation and navigation canals throughout British India. Captain Cotton experimented to upgrade and invent new uses of the machine, documented in detail by his daughter.
[9]Knight Commander of the Order of the Star of India

2

ANCESTORS OF INDIAN RAILWAYS
Beyond the Beginnings

THE RED HILLS RAILWAY

The Red Hills are called so because of the colour of their soil and rocks. Around 1836, the construction of a rudimentary railway line was started in these hills within the city of Madras to carry hard laterite used as road-building material. It was completed a year later, in 1837. The line, though basic and experimental, remains the oldest documented railway in India today. Makeshift trains actually ran and ferried people on this line, and even though they were mostly workers, it was considered a success. The 16 January 1838 edition of the *Madras Herald* gives an interesting account of a self-propelled train, run with the help of wind-powered rotary machines.[10]

---

[10]Simon Darwill, 'India's First Railways,' Dec 2011, http://www.irfca.org/docs/history/india-first-railways.html

The following is an excerpt:

We had another most gratifying sail on the Red Hill Railway last Monday afternoon. There was a modest breeze from the N by E, and as the road runs very nearly at right angles, or E by S and W by N, the wind was favourable going and returning. The carriage is a small conveyance fitted up with springs; it is large enough to carry four or five persons, and is furnished with a small lug sail. The wheels are low, and in some places the road has suffered much by the last monsoon, yet in spite of these obstacles, the carriage travelled at least twelve miles an hour; and when the wind freshened, it was necessary to ease off the sheet to prevent the vehicle going at a greater velocity than would be agreeable, or, in the present state of the rails, safe.

The line was closed by 1845. But it was on these lines that Captain Cotton conducted several experiments with the rotary steam-powered engines, attaching carriages and ferrying people.[11] This line, because of the runs on it, indisputably remains the documented ancestor of the Indian Railways.

The experiments were first conducted at the lower Annicut (an irrigation weir) across the Coleroon river,

---

[11]The trials were documented in January 1839 by Captain John Thomas Smith in *Reports, Correspondence and Original Papers on Various Professional Subjects Connected with the Duties of Corps of Engineers of Madras Presidency—vol.1*

close to Trichinopoly, and later at the Porto Novo Iron Works, once located on the Coromandel coast. The trials were documented a year later (January 1839) by Captain John Thomas Smith in an official and private compilation titled *Reports, Correspondence and Original Papers on Various Professional Subjects Connected with the Duties of Corps of Engineers of Madras Presidency*.

The object of the proposal, writes Captain Smith in the preface of the compilation, was to provide a record of the experience of its several members for the benefit of all and 'keep up a more lively interest in duties'.

In a chapter titled 'Notes of Some Experiments Made by Captain A. Cotton, upon Mr Avery's Steam Engine', Captain Smith says he managed to lay his hands on a few of the experimentation notes by A.T. Cotton and published them for wider use. Some excerpts below might be useful to the reader.

> A great variety of highly interesting experiments have been lately made by Captain A. Cotton, on the subject of the efficiency of Mr Avery's Steam Engine, and its fitness for locomotive, and other purposes in India.

He notes the technicalities of the new find and its method of usage.

THE FIRST EXPERIMENTS OF THE 'NEW MECHANICAL AGENT'

The first experiments which were made on this engine were tried at the lower Annicut (irrigation weir) across the

Coleroon,[12] about 35 miles below Trichinopoly.[13]

> A small machine was here made for pounding of
> magnesia, and by it a hammer weighing 30 lbs was
> tilted by the usual contrivance of a set of wipers
> fixed on the circumference of a cylinder, which was
> made to turn by a strap passing around a large band
> wheel fixed on it, and over a pulley on the same axle
> with arms. The boiler which supplied this engine was
> ascertained by experiments, to evaporate about ¾ of a
> cubic foot of water per hour, which was made use of in
> the condition of steam of 30 lbs, effective pressure...[14]

But this experiment, conducted on a small scale, was
not enough to generalize the results. Larger experiments
continued being administered at the Porto Novo Iron Works.

TRIAL AT PORTO NOVO IRON WORKS

The next trial of which I have any notes was made
at Porto Novo. Here, a pair of arms was fitted to a
common boiler, the evaporating power of which was
not measured, but was estimated by the engineer
(Mr Brunton) to be sufficient to supply a 5 horsepower

---

[12]Coleroon is today's Kollidam river that is the northern distributary of
the Kaveri river and it flows through the delta of Thanjavur.

[13]Trichinopoly covers the present-day districts of Tiruchirappalli, Karur,
Ariyalur and Perambalur in the Indian state of Tamil Nadu.

[14]J.T. Smith, 'Notes of some experiments made by A.Cotton, upon
Mr Avery's steam engine,' *Reports, Correspondence and Original Papers on
Various Professional Subjects Connected with the Duties of Corps of Engineers
of Madras Presidency—vol.1*, pp.95–100

engine in the common way, that is, evaporating about 7 or 8 cubic feet of water per hour. At an effective pressure of 50 lbs, the arms, which were each 30 inches long, and of a circular form 1¼ inches diameter, attained a speed of 1,000 revolutions per minute, indicating a velocity at their extremities of 15,708 feet, without any load.[15]

> The next memorandum which I come to is a valuable experiment on the issue of steam. It is contained in the following extract dated 5 May 1838.

Experiment on 5 May 1838:

> By a very careful experiment continued for an hour and thirty minutes, I obtained a constant pressure at the end of the arms of 2¼ lbs at 40 lbs (effective) pressure per square inch—diameter of orifices ³/₁₆ inch each, or area of both ¹/₁₂ square inch.

The experiment was repeated the same month with another pair of arms and it worked very well.

Experiment on 31 May 1838:

> On 31 May another pair of arms was attached to a large boiler, whose evaporating power was estimated to be equal to about 41 cubic feet per hour; there was therefore calculated to remain 10 cubic feet per hour for the supply of the arms. The greatest velocity obtained by this engine was from 15 to 18,000 feet

---

[15]Smith, 'Steam Engine,' 95–100

per minute; and by way of trial, an iron lathe was attached to it, which 'worked very well'.

Finally, a locomotive!

While these experiments were being made, another small engine was in progress at the Red Hills. It was originally constructed as a locomotive, to run on the railway between that point and Madras, but its power was found insufficient for that purpose.

Experiments were conducted on this engine and sufficient knowledge was derived from the results obtained to show that the evaporating power of a boiler capable of keeping up the required force at the end of the arms must be much greater than the one tried; and it also seemed to be a fair conclusion from the whole of the trials made, that 8–10 oz. per cubic foot of water evaporated per hour, was the utmost that could be safely calculated on.

A new locomotive engine was now constructed from the above data; and, as it was considered that a force of 3 lbs at the end of the arms would be amply sufficient for the purpose required, such a capacity was given to the boiler as to ensure an evaporating power of about 4 or 5 cubic foot per hour. This was completed in the latter end of August 1838, after a few preliminary trials.[16]

The data above is sufficient evidence that a new locomotive engine was constructed. The train, with the locomotive,

---

[16]Smith, 'Steam Engine,' 95–100

carriages and passengers, was scheduled for a trial run on 28 August 1838.

INDIA'S FIRST TRAIN FERRYING PEOPLE, 1838

Sir Arthur Thomas Cotton's experiments on rotary steam engines seemed to be making headway. Enough data had been gathered and a new locomotive engine was finally constructed from the variation trials of the stationary steam engine. The new engine was ready for a trial run, with carriages and people, waiting to be ferried on the Red Hills Railway.

Experiment 1: Four-car Train at 2.5 Miles Per Hour

The first experiment was conducted on Tuesday, 28 August 1838. It has been documented under the heading 'Experiment No. 1 with Locomotive'.

The technical specifications of the locomotive were as follows: It had three-foot-long arms[17] with a thickness of 1/5th inch. The weight of the engine and carriage was 2,800 lbs. Three other carriages, with an additional weight of 3,000 lbs, were attached. The coal and water, along with other stuff, added up to about 600 lbs. Twenty-one persons occupied the carriages.

The total weight of the train—including the engine, four carriages, coal and water, and twenty-one persons— totalled up to 8,800 lbs, or 4 tonnes.

---

[17]The arms mean the piston rods here.

The train plied at a speed of about 2.5 miles per hour.

Experiment 2: Two-car Train at 3.5 Miles Per Hour

The second train experiment on the Red Hills Railway was conducted on the same day and it ferried two carriages and ten persons.

It had the same technical specifications as that of the first train, except for the fact that this one possessed a comparatively reduced total weight of 6,500 lbs, since it had just two carriages (weighing about 2,000 lbs) and ten people (weighing about 1,200 lbs).

Being lighter, this train was faster and had a speed of 3.5 miles per hour.

Experiment 3: Only the Engine with Two People on an Incline

The third experiment on the same day was conducted on an ascending path with an inclination of 1 in 60[18] and steam at 30 lbs. It had no carriages attached, just the steam engine with two persons. This had the reduced total weight of 3,200 lbs, and it attained a speed of 3.5 miles per hour.

The report stated that in these experiments, the total force exerted at the end of the arm was much less than what was calculated. This was owing to defects in the furnace and the chimney, which produced an insufficient draught.

---

[18]This is an engineering colloquial of a gradient or a slope.

Hence it was impossible to keep up a proper fire. These defects were soon remedied and the power subsequenty increased—finally sufficient to propel the engine at an increased speed.

EXPERIMENTS LEAD TO IMPROVIZATION!

The next set of experiments whose records are available were conducted on Wednesday, 12 September 1838. These were for a heavier engine and train, with eight passengers, at 4.5 miles per hour. The technical specifications were a bit altered, with the engine, the boiler and the carriage weighing 3,000 lbs (as against the earlier 2,800 lbs), the tender or coal car and coal weighing 1,600 lbs, and a carriage with eight passengers weighing 2,400 lbs—weighing a total of 7,000 lbs, or 3.12 tonnes. The pressure in the boiler was about 50 lbs. The whole train moved at the rate of about 4½ miles per hour, the highest speed achieved so far. The road where this experiment was conducted was not very level; there was an ascent of about one foot in a thousand.

It is known from the paper about the locomotives that experiments ceased abruptly after the second test, as Captain Cotton, the driving force behind the experiments and the railway, became ill.

Smith writes:

> ...It is much to be regretted that abrupt termination of experiments by the sudden departure of their indefatigable author, owing to ill health, has deprived us of the opportunity of becoming acquainted with

the results of a further prosecution of the enquiry in the capabilities of this machine. This is the more unfortunate, since the most important question relative to it, viz. its comparative efficiency as a mechanical agent with the other means of applying steam now in use, rests upon the determination of a point still left undecided.[19]

The Madras government, in a public citation dated October 1838, recognized Captain Cotton's development of a 'rotatory' engine. Captain Cotton left on sick leave for Tasmania on 12 December 1838. He returned to India in October 1840 briefly, and then finally in April 1843 for good. During an experiment with his engine soon after his arrival in Hobart in 1838, Cotton had been seriously injured by an explosion of the boiler. He was unable to walk for months. His influence in Tasmania helped in irrigation gaining acceptance as an aid to cereal production and the livestock industry, and for developing various apparatus for the same, including a steam-driven digging machine.[20]

The Red Hills Railway was left incomplete and was eventually shut down after Captain Cotton left, but the experiments stated above gave him an important insight into building and running railway lines, helping him in the completion of the canal work along the Godavari.

---

[19]Smith, 'Steam Engine,' 95–100
[20]'Arthur Cotton and Irrigation in Tasmania', *Papers and Proceedings of the Royal Society of Tasmania.*(Hobart: The Society, 1985), p.119

'Circumstances arose, which prevented the completion of the line, but it afforded practical experience, which was of considerable use to him in the execution of the Godavari works years after, where railway lines played an important part in facilitating the prompt construction of the great dams,' quotes his daughter in his biography.[21]

Captain Cotton eventually returned to India and the Madras Corps of Engineers, and by mid-1844, had been given charge of irrigation works on the Godavari, where a large railway was built under his supervision to facilitate the work.

Porto Novo Iron Works became the Indian Steel and Iron Company in 1833 and suffered severe losses. It became the East India Iron Company in 1853—formed primarily by merchants, and the efforts to revive the company continued until they were finally given up in 1874, when the company went into liquidation.[22]

ROORKEE'S LOCOMOTIVE THOMASON

Another experiment that failed but remains documented in India's railway history is the arrival of the locomotive Thomason. This took place in another part of the country, about two decades after the Bombay experiments, but before the first official train started running. Its story

---

[21]Elizabeth Reid (Cotton) Hope, *General Sir Arthur Cotton: His Life and Work*, William Digby, 1900

[22]Radhe Shyam Rungta, Brief History of the Iron and Steel Industry in India (Appendix 5), *Rise of Business Corporations in India: 1851–1900* (Cambridge University Press, 1970), p.276

began in north India, in 1851. Plans for regular railway lines in India had been cleared by the English Parliament, and upbeat companies that had been set up were in the process of constructing railway lines—at Bombay in the west and Howrah in the east—when what can be referred to as the 'first-of-its-kind' steam locomotive quietly made its way into the subcontinent to assist the canal works along the Ganges. The Ganges Canal Works was a large-scale irrigation project that commenced in 1845. As part of this project, an aqueduct was constructed to carry the Solani river water across the Ganges canal at Roorkee. The locomotive arrived here and was named Thomason—after the Lieutenant Governor of the North-west Provinces at the time, James Thomason. It ran successfully for sometime but eventually died due to a blast in its boiler. Evidence suggests that after this incident it worked as a stationary machine for canal work.

The life and times of the locomotive Thomason and the railway that was built to facilitate the canal work are discussed in detail by Sir Proby T. Cautley, the director of the Ganges Canal Works, in the second volume of his detailed three-volume 'Report on the Ganges canal works from their commencement until the opening of the canal in 1854', on the construction of the canal. The locomotive Thomason lived a short life—from December 1851 until April 1852.

However, the locomotive proved to be helpful during the short period in which it functioned, as Captain Cautley, at one point, says, 'During the month of April, the work of the locomotive has shown a considerable improvement, and once the engine had brought 114 loads during a day. But during this operation, the working of the locomotive was stopped.'[23] A table next to this description states that the locomotive worked only for ten days in April 1852, drawing 687 loads, carrying 34,350 cubic feet of earth and running for about 14,000 feet.

Follwing is the interesting description of the railway system along the canals—its utility, the locomotive and its death—in Captain Cautley's own words.[24]

THE SYSTEM

A system of railways, connected with the brick manufactories which had been established at Roorkee and Muhewur, that is to say, at each end of the aqueduct. The railways were necessarily a main feature in the earthen aqueduct, as it was through their aid that the embankments would be formed.

THE FIRST RAILS

The first rail that was laid consisted of bars of flat iron, varying from ¼ to ¾ inch thickness, screwed

---

[23] Radhe Shyam Rungta, 'Brief History of the Iron and Steel Industry,' p.448.

[24] Proby T. Cautley, 'Solani Aqueduct,' *Report on the Ganges Canal Works from Their Commencement until the Opening of the Canal in 1854, vol.2,* ch.9, pp.411–537

upon longitudinal sleepers, which held in position by cross-bars or transoms. In 1850, however, 30,000 running feet of light rail bars, which had been selected in England by Major Baker, arrived at the works.

THE LOCOMOTIVE

On 22 December 1851, we started a locomotive, which I believe must have been the first engine of the sort that was ever used in India. The engine was in some way or other imperfect in the adjustment of its parts; it was continually getting out of order, and appeared to be another specimen of machinery for exportation to the colonies. The locomotive is small and compact; engine and tender in one frame; adapted from its water fuel arrangements to moderate distances only, and applicable to draw on a level line of rail, a train of ballast of wagons of an aggregate weight of 180 to 200 tonnes at a speed of four miles an hour. Of the parts most liable to fracture, we have duplicates, as well as of the wheels, both driving, tail, and leading. Its name is the 'Thomason'. The executive engineer in charge of the Northern Division of the works, in writing to me on the subject of its applicability for the particular duties which the aqueduct works required from it, remarked: 'The locomotive started first on 22 December 1851, at the Roorkee end of the railway.'

THE WAGONS

A number of small wagons made up with side doors and without tilting apparatus arrived at Roorkee. These gave us the early means of commencing our earth-carrying operations. I had, however, brought with me from England tracings of what I thought to be the wagon best adapted to our works (with rear tilting), with the ironwork of one wagon complete.

FREEDOM FROM WHEELBARROWS AND BASKETS

The introduction of railroads and wagons relieved us from wheelbarrows and baskets, but for a long time kept us with men both for excavation and for propelling the wagons. As time advanced, horses in some measure took the place of men; and on 22 December 1851, we started a locomotive, which I believe to have been the first engine of the sort that was ever used in India. We, therefore, went through all the grades of carriage, with varied results, all of which, however, appeared to be dependent on local causes, or economical arrangements with regard to time.

Our methods of working, therefore, were:
First, with baskets and wheelbarrows
Second, with earth-wagons propelled by men
Third, with earth-wagons propelled by horses
Fourth, with earth-wagons propelled by a locomotive.

THE DEATH

The sad death of the locomotive is referred in passing while discussing the calculation of rates and quantity of earth ferried in the fourth method of working.

> On the fourth item, our experience in rates of earth as obtained by the use of a locomotive was too short to admit of our arriving at any satisfactory conclusions, an accident having placed the machine hors de combat a few months after it had been on the works. The water had been drawn off and it was supposed that the fire had been entirely extinguished. A storm with wind, however, brought the fire and fuel which were in the furnace into action, destroyed the casing, together with a number of the tubes, and placed the locomotive completely out of use.[25]

It is not clear if the locomotive was ever revived for the runs, but it most probably ended up as a stationary engine along the canal works. But such raw experiments make for important documentation of how they tried to utilize steam power for locomotion. It also gives us an insight into how such trials gave a first-hand experience to the Indians of the generation at various levels and in various parts of the subcontinent. Every new experiment led to improvization and added finesse. The era of the Indian Railways had begun!

---

[25]Proby T. Cautley, 'Solani Aqueduct,' pp.411–537

3

RAILWAYS BEGIN THEIR OPERATIONS
A Race to the Finish

LAYING THE FOUNDATION

What we read in the earlier chapters were details of early experiments, which, when documented, help stitch together India's railway history.

Since the 1830s, there were experiments at various levels with rail tracks and steam power. In the 1840s, in line with the developments in England and many other countries, railway lines were proposed to be laid in India, with parliamentarians and business tycoons lobbying for or against it. The challenge was to make them financially viable and sustainable—with most businessmen wanting guaranteed returns on investment, and the planners and strategists wanting the railways to be a vital means of imports and of military importance. Long-drawn debates and documentation took place. The key subject of dispute on the table was that after the huge investments of construction and operation, would the 'natives' accept this new development at all? Would there be substantial returns? The construction of railway lines across an unfamiliar terrain came with an element of risk. The promoters were confident, but there were wary officials and a few parliamentarians who remained divided in their opinion. There were, of course, profits to be made.

A paper presented in October 1847 before the House of Commons discussed trade relations between India and England, focussing specifically on cotton. Cotton, it said, grew in the interiors of India, in places without transport and communication facilities. Therefore, by the time it reached the country's shores from the villages, it got damaged, thanks to the unreliable transport network, i.e., chiefly bullock carts. Worse, during times of drought and famine, the bullock carts got further delayed; on such occasions, ships were kept waiting at ports for goods that never arrived. With a rail line, things would change drastically. Cotton, and indeed every raw material, would get transported with remarkable speed to the sea ports. From there, the cotton could be sent by ship to Britain and its hungry textile mills. Back then, cotton, a crucial commodity for the textile industry in the United Kingdom (UK), was mainly purchased from America. Though India, too, used to export cotton, the quantities were minuscule. However, Britain did not want to be dependent exclusively on America for cotton, and from the 1840s, showed deep interest in cotton cultivation in India.

J.A. Turner, resident of the Manchester Commercial Association, in fact wrote a letter in 1847 that clearly explained the aim of establishing the railways.

> I believe that if Indian cotton is sent home clean, there will be an increased demand for it; and that it is very unlikely that the spinners will discontinue using it, even if American cotton recedes from its present value; though of course they would, in such cases, only use it at its relative value compared with the American.[26]

Another need for a faster mode of transport was military might. It was a fact that besides giving the growing native population better mobility, railways would enable faster deployment of troops.

Besides cotton trade, military use of the railway line would prove of immense benefit, and a letter[27] to that effect written by Thomas Williamson, Revenue Commissioner of Bombay, to the chairman of the Great Indian Peninsular Railway (GIPR) company, Lord Wharncliffe, in May 1846, is self-explanatory. He recommended an alignment through the Malshej Ghats.

---

[26]John Chapman, 'Quality of Indian Cotton,' *The Cotton and Commerce of India, Considered in Relation to the Interests of Great Britain with Remarks on Railway Communication in the Bombay Presidency*, London (Jan 1851) chap.1, p.8.

[27]Thomas Williamson, 'Two Letters on the Advantages of Railway Communication in Western India,' Richard and John E. Taylor, eds., Fleet Street, 1846

I need not remind your Lordship that Bombay is the great focus of our military strength in western India. Its admirable harbour, at the most centrical [*sic*] point on the west coast of the Peninsula, has since the time of our first connection with India, pointed it out as the key of our possessions in this quarter. There are our Dockyards, our Arsenals, our Manufactories of Ordnance and other stores; and it is the only point on the whole coast where troops can, at all times of the year, be embarked and disembarked without difficulty or delay.

In Europe, the importance of a railway as a military work is limited to the speed and comfort with which large bodies of troops may be conveyed to their destination; but in India its value is enhanced by the mode in which it would spare the health and save the lives of European troops.

Should an arrangement at any future time be concluded for the passage of troops through Egypt, the importance of the Great Indian Peninsula Railway would be vastly increased.

The great trunk line, running by the Malseje Ghaut in the direction of Nagpoor, would be the most direct which could possibly be selected to connect Bombay and Calcutta.

Such reports were slowly tilting the scales in favour of the railways. The debate finally ended with a 'push' from Governor General James Andrew Broun-Ramsay, First Marquess of Dalhousie, or simply Lord Dalhousie. (He was the Governor General of India between 12 January 1848 and 28 February 1856.) A fan of the railways, he drew up a map and wrote minutes on how improving internal communication in India was important and how the railways would play a key role in it. The minutes are today a central document of Indian Railways' history. A key directive for construction was to refrain from embellishments for station infrastructure. Unlike stations in England, there was to be no extravaganza, only simple stations and railway tracks. Thus, the process of introducing the railways into the subcontinent began. India was now at a crucial juncture, where its primary mode of transport— carts and carriages drawn by oxen or horses—was set to change for good. The age of the railways was about to dawn.

Howrah and Bombay, on the eastern and the western coasts respectively, were in the race to get the first railway line. It was the talking point locally, and one of the most discussed topics in periodicals and at public gatherings, with merchants and traders from both these places trying to take the lead, forming associations, gaining backing and building public support to further their cause. Surveys and studies were conducted. Among the public, there was curiosity, questions, calculations and, of course, superstitions. 'What if...?' was the common beginning for the most frequently asked questions. The key question was the same as was discussed earlier—whether it would be profitable to those who were investing in it heavily. The masses, of course, considered it evil, as they couldn't imagine how a fire-spitting metal could have a life of its own and run a few hundred kilometres.

However, once the idea was formalized, the processes of formation moved speedily. The Bill to incorporate the GIPR on the western coast came up before the Parliament in England in March 1847. It was initially withdrawn after opposition from the East India Company over certain clauses, but was re-tabled two years later, on 1 August 1849, and was cleared. Soon, a formal contract was signed on 17 August 1849 between the East India Company and the GIPR to lay a 21–mile 'Experimental Line of Railway' from Bombay to Thane.

On the eastern front, it was Rowland MacDonald Stephenson who submitted to the East India Company the first traffic and engineering feasibility report for a line from Calcutta to Mirzapore, leading to the establishment of the East Indian Railway (EIR) Company in May 1845. He became the first agent and managing director of the EIR. Four years later, a contract was signed to construct and operate a 161–km–long 'Experimental Line' between Calcutta and Rajmahal, which would later be extended to Delhi via Mirzapore.

As both companies raced to complete their lines, a few dramatic incidents, a combination of ill luck, miscalculation and land issues led to the delay of the east coast line. In the end, Bombay won a dramatic victory.

CHALLENGES THAT THE ENGLISH ENGINEERS DID NOT FORESEE

The plan to build the rail lines taking into account all kinds of pressure groups, individual promoters, survey reports and arguments both in favour of and against the construction of railways in India seemed to have failed to deal with all aspects of railway construction here.

That is not to say that the planning was not detailed. One would be surprised to read old records on how meticulous the British were and how thoroughly they conducted their research and planning, to the extent that a few administrators, promoters and investors went on to calculate the return of every penny invested in the proposed railways in India. It was a practical approach to building a practical railway. But the problem was not just related to engineering on unfamiliar terrain. There were problems of harsh weather conditions and related complexities, rigid local customs, superstitions that sometimes led to grave issues and lack of know-how at the grass-roots level, as it was the first time that something like a railroad was being set up on a large scale.

One official letter written by a director of the East India Company to the Governor General of India lists six reasons why the railways in India were thought to be difficult to lay, due to 'peculiarities of the climate and circumstances' of the country and how they should first be tried on a limited scale. The *Railway Register Journal* published in London in 1845 wrote an article reproducing the letter and adding the following 'practical' reasons to curtail the scale of the operation in its list.[28]

CURIOUS DIFFICULTIES IN BUILDING RAILWAYS FOR INDIA: RAINS, INSECTS AND MORE

The physical obstacles which are to be overcome or neutralized before a system of railways can be carried into execution in India, have, to a certain extent, been foreseen and pointed out by the East India directors, in their letter of the 7th of May last, addressed to the Governor General of India. In that letter, they observe, 'Independent of the difficulties common to railroads in all countries, there are others peculiar to the climate and circumstances of India, which may render it advisable that the first attempt should be made upon a limited scale.

These difficulties may be classed under the following heads:

1. Periodical rains and inundations
2. The continued action of violent winds and influence of a vertical sun
3. The ravages of insects and vermin upon timber and earthwork
4. The destructive effects of the spontaneous vegetation of underwood upon earth and brickwork

---

[28] *Railways in India; Being Four Articles Reprinted from the Railway Register for July, August, September, and November, 1845* (London: Madden And Malcom, 1845)

5. The unenclosed and unprotected tracts of country through which railroads would pass
6. The difficulty and expense of securing the services of competent and trustworthy engineers

These obstacles, combined with the entire want of definite and scientific information relative to the applicability of railway communication to India, have induced the Company to take the step to which reference has been already made, that of employing a qualified engineer to survey the country, in order to fix upon the most eligible lines which might be available for the experiment.

PECULIARITIES FOR THE FIRST RAILWAY ENGINEERS

The *Railway Register* went on to add a few more 'peculiarities' of which the first railway engineers in India should be careful, which could turn cities to ruins. These were to be kept in mind by all those who attempted to carry out the work for the railway system in the country. Apart from the physical impediments that were mentioned, the following difficulties were also to be considered:

First: The difficulties which the instability of soil itself presents
Second: The impediments which the variations in the surface offer, these presenting features of a character wholly distinct from the ordinary difficulties which

present themselves in climates and regions such as those of France, England and other European countries.

Frequent Earthquakes

India is a very different country: what constitutes the exception in more temperate climes forms unhappily the rule there, as any one may ascertain by referring to the meteorological history of that continent for the last half century, within which time only European observations have been regularly conducted. It is a notorious fact that there seldom a month passes during certain seasons of the year, in which the shock of an earthquake is not felt in one part of India or another; not often, we admit, so severe as to crumble cities into ruins.[29]

Rain and Sun

The second of the peculiar local obstacles to which we have alluded consists in the various and uncertain nature of the surface upon which the rails are to be laid.

---

[29] *Wide Bombay Transactions, vol.3*. pp.96–101. The article cited details of the 1819 earthquake. 'That of 1819, however, destroyed upwards of 2,000 persons, and levelled to the ground the principal part of the towns of Bhuoj, Anjar, Mothora, Thera, Kotheree, Wulliah, Mandree, and Luckput; besides damaging many forts and other large works. The effects of this earthquake were distinctly felt in a range embracing a space of 18° latitude and 20° of longitude, extending to Calcutta on the east, Catmandoo on the north, Pondicherry to the south, and the mountains of Beloochistan to the west.'

We need hardly remind the reader of the well-known fact that during four months in the year the whole country is annually subjected to an inundation which covers its surface to a depth varying from 18 inches to several feet, according to its level; as we approach the uplands the continuous rains form water-courses, rushing with irresistible rapidity, and carrying all before them occasionally.

During the hot and cold months respectively, these water courses are dried up, forming ravines, which, in the case of a high road being carried in their direction, are necessarily bridged over.

In general, the traffic roads in Hindostan are merely the dried-up beds of water courses, and when the periodical rains commence, of course travelling by land-carriages ceases.[30]

HOWRAH: THE BEGINNINGS

How Sinking Ships and Land Issues Delayed the East India Railway Operations

The first official passenger railway line in India was opened by the GIPR between the 21-mile stretch of Bori Bunder and Thane on 16 April 1853, with trials held a year earlier. The East Indian line seemed a bit ahead—with 38 miles of tracks in place by 1853—but two mishaps left it without

---

[30] *Railways in India; Being Four Articles Reprinted from the Railway Register for July, August, September, and November, 1845* (London: Madden And Malcom, Leaden Hall Street, 1845)

rail cars or locomotives and prevented the running of the first train. It opened formally, in phases, a year later, starting 1 September 1854.

The ship HMS Goodwin, which was carrying the first railway carriages for the EIR, sank at Sandheads near Diamond Harbour, at the mouth of the Hooghly. Sandheads has been documented as a very dangerous area and only an expert sailor could navigate it safely. This left the railways without carriages, and since the arrival of another set would take weeks, they were made locally. This was both faster and cheaper, and the coaches could be customized this way. Mr John Hodgson, the Chief Locomotive Engineer, East Indian Railway, started the process, but it was eventually completed by two Calcutta-based coach-building firms—Messrs Stewart and Company, and Seton and Company. However, the locomotives or engines arriving for the EIR also met a somewhat similar fate. An archival report states that the ship carrying the locomotives went to the continent of Australia instead of reaching India.[31] Finally, the locomotive reached Calcutta via Australia by HMS Dekagree in 1854, but by then, it was too late to compete with Bombay. The first passenger train had been run in Bombay a year earlier and the EIR had missed making history!

On 28 June 1854, Mr Hodgson and his team took a trial trip from Howrah to Pundooah. The railway was

---

[31]Anuradha Kumar, 'Two Men and a Railway Line—Steam Power, the Opium Trade, and Calcutta of the 1840s,' IRFCA, 2013, http://www.irfca.org/articles/two-men-railway-line.html

opened as far as Hooghly, a distance of 24 miles, on 15 August, and up to Pundooah on 1 September 1854. On Saturday, 3 February 1855, the line was opened up to Raniganj, as originally planned.[32]

The delays in opening the sections were due to a few other reasons too. There was a boundary problem with France, as Chandernagore was under French control, and tracks were found to be encroaching on its boundary. Further, the line was reported to have displaced houses, gardens and even religious structures, generating opposition, which delayed the opening of the line.

The following four news reports of that time give a peek into the town's public sentiment and how difficult it must have been for the railway workers on the ground to get the work done.

'No Compensation'

The *Calcutta Chronicle* learns that the 'first sod' of the Great Indian Railway has been actually turned; and the work commenced in right earnest. Trees, plants, houses, that seemed to have fallen within the line of the expected railroad, are now being removed, and the inhabitants of the neighbouring villages at Bailee, Wooterparah, Sulkeah[33] & C., are loud in their complaints, as no compensation is now offered them for the injuries sustained in consequence. The

---

[32]J.N. Sahni, 'The Beginning,' *Indian Railways—One Hundred Years (1853-1953)*, Ministry of Railways (1953), chap.1, p.5
[33]Bally, Uttarpara, Salkia

local magistrates say they do not entertain complaints proffered against the railway pioneers, but recommend them to apply to the government on the subject of the damages done.

Woman in Childbirth Not Spared

The Hurkaru states that the railway contractors have already cleared the line between Howrah and Serampore, but heavy complaints are made by the native population, whose property, it seems, has been sacrificed without due notice, and in a very harsh manner. In one case even a poor woman in the agonies of childbirth was denied one night's delay. We would fain hope that these accounts are grossly exaggerated. The worst feature of the case, as represented, is that no record is kept of the injury to individuals, so that it will be difficult for them to obtain compensation.[34]

Howrah Terminus on the Land of Captain Oakes

The railway company at Calcutta has advertised for tenders for the construction of the section of the line which extends from Pandua to Raneegunge, to commence with the approaching cold weather: for the convenience of contractors, the section was to be divided into lots of between five and six miles

---

[34]*Allen's Indian Mail and Register of Intelligence for British and Foreign India, China & All Parts of the East. vol.9*, no.164, (London, Thursday, Jan 2, 1851) p.6. A new volume was published on the arrival of each overland mail.

each. *The Hurkaru* mentions that the site of the railway terminus at Howrah has been fixed upon. The property belonging to Captain Oakes, near the Howrah Ghaut, is the place selected.[35]

Landlord Holds Up Railway Works

The railway has, it appears, been brought to a stand for the present from the opposition offered by a wealthy landholder (Goopee Kistna Gossain, of Serampore) to the invasion of his grounds without legal authority. Great blame attaches somewhere for the delay which has occurred in providing such authority. A commissioner has been appointed for obtaining and making over the land required, but he cannot interfere till empowered by a legislative enactment, and the necessary Act, which ought to have been Law months since, and was some time ago promulgated in draft, has not yet been passed. There have been great complaints of the harsh and summary proceedings of the 'railway pioneers' to the poor people along the line, who found their houses pulled down about their ears without a moment's notice.[36]

Work Paces Ahead

The *Friend of India* announces, with the most unfeigned satisfaction, that the first inch of the

---

[35] *Allen's Indian Mail, vol.9*, no.181, (London, Friday, September 19, 1851), pp.538–539.

[36] *Allen's Indian Mail, vol.9*, no.165, (London, Friday, Jan 17, 1851), p.36.

ground was made over to the railway establishment on the 25th of January, 'one year, two months, and eleven days after the despatch of the letter from the Court of Directors, in which they twice enforced the necessity of accelerating this preliminary measure'.

The *Morning Chronicle* states that at Balikal at least nine hundred coolies were busily at work every day at the railway embankments, which were rapidly rising. The *Roshoshagar*, a native paper, indicates some of the peculiar difficulties which these works will encounter in India.

On account of the famous Musjeed of the Pandooah falling within the boundary of the railway line, a show of resistance and violence had been offered by the good Mussulmans of the place towards the railway people when they expressed a desire of levelling it to the ground, adding that the British government must first extirpate them before they break down their place of worship. The magistrate of Hooghly, with a company of native infantry, went to the spot, and the whole hubbub was soon at an end.[37]

---

[37] *Allen's Indian Mail, vol. 9*, no.169, (London, Saturday, March 22, 1851), p.154

BOMBAY: THE BEGINNINGS

Clash of Cultures, Strike and Superstition

There were strikes and protests in Bombay by native workers for better facilities such as better timings and hot water for bath. The English had clearly not foreseen this. But eventually, as the workers settled, the work proceeded smoothly.

The first Bombay contractors, William Fredrick Faviell and Henry Fowler, were experienced hands in England. They sailed to India on 19 December 1850. They got down to work immediately by employing nearly 10,000 workers, a largely rural workforce gathered from various neighbouring districts.

Invincible Prejudices

It was for the very first time that British engineers were dealing with native workers for a railway project. It was a clash of two cultures, with British engineers focussing on making the labour effective and the workers, in turn, demanding respect for their methods and religious practices.

Professor Ian J. Kerr, in his book *Building the Railways of the Raj: 1850-1900*, documents how a harried Mr Fowler shot off a letter on 2 May 1851 to his mentor in England stating that he had been trying to get the workers to start work at 6 a.m. instead of the customary 8 a.m., but 'it is a most difficult thing to alter the existing system, as almost every custom the natives have is founded on absurd but invincible prejudices—generally of religious character'.[38]

Fowler lamented how the workers' groups were divided into castes, affecting work, as they often would not work alongside men of other castes, and gives an example of how the workers had destroyed a vessel because Fowler had used it for a while.[39]

Rigid Work Practices

The *Bombay Quarterly Review* of July-October 1855 reports a strike by railway workers at the Coorla cutting for change in work timings so that they could take a hot water bath. It is not clear if this was the same episode that Fowler had been referring to and was reported by *The Review Magazine*. But the excerpts are indeed interesting!

> In the month of November soon after the commencement of the Coorla cutting, a deputation of native workmen waited upon the contractor with a complaint about the hours of working, which were then from 8 a.m. to 6 p.m. They solicited their master to allow them to begin their day an hour earlier, so that they might leave work before sunset, because at 6 o'clock the water was too cold for them to bathe.[40]

[38]Ian J. Kerr, *Building the Railways of the Raj*, Oxford University Press, 1995

[39]Rajendra B. Aklekar, 'The Story of an Experimental Line,' *Halt Station India: The Dramatic Tale of the Nation's First Rail Lines* (Rupa Publications, 2015), pp.8–9

[40]Ibid

Yet another story states how one day in the 1850s, during the construction of the line, there was a sudden strike by workers due to a lack of assurance on wages: 'One day, the engineer who was engaged at Sion was surprised to observe all the native labourers from the large cutting in that neighbourhood were walking away as no one had assured them of payment. Only when the engineer guaranteed them the wages did they turn around.'[41]

Relations between native labourers, contractors and British engineers remained strained. Conditions worsened when the line reached the difficult Bhore Ghat near the Khandala stretch between Bombay and Pune in the 1850s. This was a tough mountainous stretch, with the worst possible working conditions, leading to wage disputes, illness, injuries, riots, sickness and thousands of deaths, which eventually led the British to enforce a law and despatch a full-fledged police force on the line to handle difficult situations. The Employers' and Workmen's (Disputes) Act (X) implemented in 1860 gave powers to magistrates to settle wage disputes.

Land issues, religious disputes, boundary problems, strikes over hot water and what not! All this, despite the railway planners in India being painstakingly thorough in their work.

Despite all such odds and unpredictable hurdles, the lines were finally ready, up and running, and what came next was another set of complexities—and that too very

---

[41] *The Bombay Quarterly Review,* July–October 1855.

'Hindustanee'. Read on to experience the sometimes hilarious and sometimes serious issues the population using the railways in India faced.

4

THE ARRIVAL OF THE RAILWAYS
A Danav, Agni Rath, Time Travel and What Not

A RAKSHAS

The sight of the first locomotive and its run led to hysteria amidst the local population. No one was sure what it was—a devil, a machine, a magical animal or some wizard that would capture their land. People hid from it, saw glimpses of it and floated stories about it. Some brave people ventured out to view and touch it. At Hooghly, a businessman flogged his horse to achieve the speed of steam trains. At another place near the Bombay railway line, there were rumours circulated that you needed to sacrifice life to power trains and the steam run required a corpse per kilometre!

In 1852, in Bombay, work on the construction of

embankments to build the line was at an advanced stage and, as Faviell and Fowler, the contractors, struggled to finish it, a steam locomotive landed at the port. It drew huge crowds and was named after the sitting Governor of Bombay, Lord Viscount Falkland. Though stationary steam machines and steam ships had been in regular use, it was the first time the people of Bombay were seeing a moving steam apparatus on rails.

Used for shunting operations, 'Lord Falkland' created euphoria. Its hissing, puffing and whistling, its smoke, soot and smell, and its sheer size and weight were awe-inspiring. From the ports, it was pulled down a public road by more than 200 coolies for its first operation. While it scared a few, it struck a chord with most others.

The engine's shunting operations began near Byculla from a grove belonging to a landlord named William Phipps. The grove, which had been cultivated with toddy trees, also had stone quarries that were later used for ballasting the railway line. As quarrying would destroy plantations, it was necessary for the railways to have absolute rights over the land to make radical changes in land use. The GIPR bought the land at a cost of ₹4,000. Phipps' land, with the engine in it, was the city's new attraction and it drew crowds from all parts of town, the site resembling a fair.

ER...WHAT TO CALL IT?

Some Indians, who had, by that time, seen a working steamship, started calling the rail engine an aag boat (a steamer), or sometimes an agni rath (a fire chariot), due to the striking similarities of smoke, soot and whistle with it. Interestingly, it was the English newspapers of the day that were at a loss for words. They debated in their periodicals on what to call the locomotive in the local language—a steam ship, a steam chariot or something more convincing.

> By what name is a railway locomotive to be known among the natives? This is not an utterly uninteresting question. They have already commenced to call her 'aag boat', which is the name given by them to a steam vessel; but this is absurd. It is suggested that the proper appellation would be 'bauf ka rutthee' [*sic*], which means a steam chariot. Now is the time to settle this important matter. If the term 'aag boat' is allowed to prevail at this time, it will infallibly stick.[42]

The debate continued. Meanwhile, the 'fair' at Byculla grounds to see the locomotive in action also attracted the attention of newspapers. The *Bombay Telegraph* dated 17 February 1852 reported:

> The native population appear to evince great interest in the 'fire chariot' as they name her, and crowd round to have a look. The weight and massive character of the whole is quite at variance with their notion

---

[42]*Allen's Indian Mail, and Register of Intelligence for British and Foreign India, China, and All Parts of the East, vol.10,* Jan–Dec 1852, p.196, quoting the *Bombay Telegraph*

of speed; and, after observing the slow progress she made when being dragged along the public road by 200 coolies, their incredulous look of astonishment is not to be wondered at, when told, that in a few days she will be able to pass the race course swifter than their fleetest Arabs.[43]

The first locomotive in action gave the native population a cultural shock. The locals, unaware of the industrial developments taking place on the other side of the world, were confident that the mechanical contraption of a running, smoke-belching steam machine pulling wagons was an all-powerful mystical creature. It gave rise to strange ideas and stranger rumours. They were confident that the monster would soon spread its ill effects on society.

A CORPSE FOR EVERY RAILWAY SLEEPER TO POWER TRAINS!

To start with, people called the train a 'lokhandi rakshas' ('iron demon' in Marathi). They maintained that no native of a high caste would ever 'defile himself by entering a railway carriage'.[44] Among the natives were also a handful of enterprising businessmen who knew the importance of the railways, its benefits and its profits. The few who were

---

[43]*Allen's Indian Mail, and Register of Intelligence for British and Foreign India, China, and All Parts of the East, vol.10,* Jan–Dec 1852, p.165, quoting the *Bombay Telegraph*

[44]S.M. Edwardes, 'Bombay, Part IV, History, 1901,' *Census of India, vol.10,* 1838–1872 Quoting *Bombay Times,* (April 16, 1853), p.120

not superstitious or ambitious about the railways simply believed it was all a cruel joke. They said that the idea of a 'steam-run machine pulling a row of wagons' was just a 'bluff' to cheat poor Indians of their land and money. The rumours refused to go away. While some said it was a ploy by the English to collect all the money from India and run away, others questioned the project, asking whether the great saints and rishi munis were fools that they had not discovered such a thing earlier. Had steam-powered locomotion really been possible, it would have been put to use much earlier. As people saw 'Lord Falkland' in action every day, another rumour was circulated that one had to bury children and young couples under the rail sleepers to power the rail engine and that the British sepoys were looking for and catching hold of every young couple and child found on the streets to put under the tracks. Yet another rumour spread was that if one travelled by rail, one's lifespan would decrease, as one would end up reaching the destination faster, fast-forwarding one's life and age![45]

But as things proceeded and the benefits of easy, clean and faster transport began to be observed, the rumours and objections died down. What had started as a means to primarily ferry cotton and goods soon became a lucrative passenger service. Edwardson's account, written in 1868 with the aid of the Records of India Office, states:

---

[45]Rajendra B. Aklekar, 'The Story of an Experimental Line,' *Halt Station India*, (Rupa Publications, 2015), chap.1

Rail markings at Royapuram station

Pillars of old rail track at Royapuram station

Royapuram station building

Early railway construction—Bombay port: 1

Courtesy: Mumbai Port Trust archives

Early railway construction—Bombay port: 2

Courtesy: Mumbai Port Trust archives

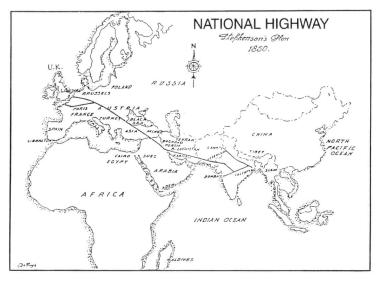

3900-mile Railway Stephenson Plan of 1850

Courtesy: J.N. Sahni, *Indian Railways—One Hundred Years: 1853-1953*

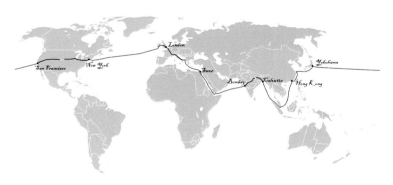

Around the world in eighty days

Courtesy: Wikimedia Commons

Train from Calcutta to Delhi passing the fortress of Rhotas
Courtesy: The *Illustrated London News*, 1851

An artillery train being loaded
Courtesy: The *Illustrated London News*, June 1875

Attack on Barwarie station

Courtesy: The *Illustrated London News*

Matheran plaque

Courtesy: Peerbhoy family book

Bullock cart train

Courtesy: Westen Railway archives

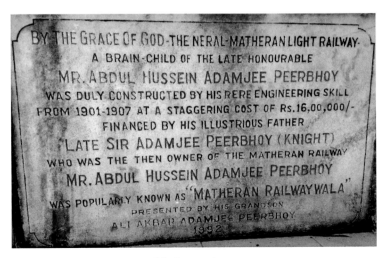

BY THE GRACE OF GOD-THE NERAL-MATHERAN LIGHT RAILWAY·
A BRAIN-CHILD OF THE LATE HONOURABLE
MR. ABDUL HUSSEIN ADAMJEE PEERBHOY
WAS DULY CONSTRUCTED BY HIS RERE ENGINEERING SKILL
FROM 1901-1907 AT A STAGGERING COST OF Rs.16,00,000/-
FINANCED BY HIS ILLUSTRIOUS FATHER
LATE SIR ADAMJEE PEERBHOY (KNIGHT)
WHO WAS THE THEN OWNER OF THE MATHERAN RAILWAY
MR. ABDUL HUSSEIN ADAMJEE PEERBHOY
WAS POPULARLY KNOWN AS "MATHERAN RAILWAYWALA"
PRESENTED BY HIS GRANDSON
ALI AKBAR ADAMJEE PEERBHOY
1992

Matheran plaque

Courtesy: Peerbhoy family book

First electric passenger train

Courtesy: Central Railway archives

First electric passenger train, front view

Courtesy: Central Railway archives

A SUTIE RELIC AT AN INDIAN RAILWAY STATION.

TALGARIA STATION PLATFORM, BENGAL-NAGPUR RAILWAY.

In the foreground, covered by the iron plates, lies the relic of a Sutie. Sutie was the custom whereby Hindu wives allowed themselves to be burnt alive on the funeral pyre of their dead husband. This spot is a sacred one. Pilgrims visit this relic, indifferent to the railway work that may be taking place.

Talgaria station

Courtesy: *The Railway Magazine*

A tiger at the station

Courtesy: Wikimedia Commons

Imperial Train at Ballard Pier

Boat trains at Ballard Pier

Courtesy: Mumbai Port Trust archives

Boat trains at Ballard Pier with troops

Courtesy: Mumbai Port Trust archives

*Chinese infantrymen being transported on a passenger train
from Kunming to Chanyi*

Courtesy: http://www.cbi-history.com/part_vi_ba_railway2.html

*Jeep train from Myitkyina arrives at the Mogaung river
and is being unloaded by members of the 775th Engineer Petroleum
Distribution Company*

Courtesy: http://www.cbi-history.com/part_vi_ba_railway2.html

MAWD engine

Courtesy: Lalam Mandavkar

Mahatma Gandhi at a railway station

Courtesy: Wikimedia Commons

Dhanushkodi—old railway station

Courtesy: Wikimedia Commons (D. Kartikeyan)

B.C. Ganguly

Courtesy: National Rail Museum archives

Konkan Railway construction

Courtesy: Konkan Railway archives

Inaugural train at Sawantwadi

Courtesy: Konkan Railway archives

One of the coaches from the 2006 Mumbai train bombings

The train after reconstruction

One of the coaches from the 2006 Mumbai train bombings

The steam engine was overturning prejudices, uprooting habits and changing customs. A man who, before railways existed, on no account would have walked or carried a pound weight, but must have had a palkhee and bearers, now cheerfully marches to the station with a carpet bag; and, strange to say, even unpunctuality and apathy vanish before the warning bell of a station master. Railways, which had gone far in England to annihilate distance, were in India to reduce to a manageable extent the vast distance of the continent; were to strengthen the government; to bind races together; and by giving an impetus to commerce, to vivify and give such a bias to the character of the peoples of India, as ages had not effected, and ages would not efface.

BIZARRE STORIES FROM THE EAST

As the first set of locomotives and carriages began working along the East India Railway in Howrah, there were equally bizarre stories and reports as in the west. A few anecdotes in J.N. Sahni's book quoting newspapers of the time captures them well. A businessman did not believe after his train journey that he had really reached his destination so fast and asked whether it would shorten his life on the whole.[46]

---

[46]J.N. Sahni, *Indian Railways: One Hundred Years, 1853-1953*, Ministry of Railways

Here's something more. Even as all this was happening, there were ambitions—and what kind! The pioneer of railways in east India, Sir Rowland, had plans not just for east India but for beyond the subcontinent. It was as early as 1843 that he brought his family to India, hoping not only to establish the railways here but extend it all the way to Europe. He conceived a plan to 'girdle the world with an iron chain' to connect Europe and Asia at their farthest extremities with one colossal railway.[47]

A 3,900-mile Railway from the English Channel to the Indus

Stephenson's plan had three phases:

i)   Connecting the railway line from the port on the English Channel in Europe to a port on the Persian Gulf, a distance of 2,800 miles, the passage to Bombay being made by steamer, and from Bombay to Calcutta by rail.

ii) Extending the line from the Persian Gulf across Persia and Baluchistan to the Indus, a distance of 1,100 miles, connecting Asia with the large railway network being developed in the subcontinent.

iii) Connecting the Indian railway network with the Chinese railway network by a link through the Nepalese range of the Himalayas up to the Tsangpo river.

---

[47]Ibid

He submitted the proposal to the East India Company, and following the inauguration of the East Indian Railway, resubmitted it to Lord Dalhousie in January 1856. Dalhousie said the project would be 'a gigantic undertaking' but conceded that once completed, it would be 'a great step in the progress of the world'.[48] He had no doubt that the East India Company would be willing, 'at the proper time', to assist, with respect to surveys and otherwise.

[48]J.N. Sahani, *Indian Railways: One Hundred Years, 1853–1953*, Ministry of Railways

5

RAIL WEB SPREADS
Bullock Carts,
the Shaitan and Rail Elephants

India's first passenger train running on the 21-mile Bombay–Thana line was a runaway success in the very first month. It was started on 16 April 1853, and regular runs began from 18 April. By 30 April, trains on this small stretch had already ferried 21,922 passengers, earning ₹9,109, 3 annas and 8 paise. By May, the number of passengers had risen to 40,071½[49] and by December to 61,413½.

WHEN BULLOCK CARTS RACED STEAM TRAINS

Traditional modes of transit began to feel the heat as trains became more and more popular. Bullock carts, for example, fell out of favour, as trains became the preferred mode of

---

[49] ½ refers to a child ticket

cargo transport. Bullock cart owners were furious. They decided to put up a fight and began charging one rate from the hinterland to Bombay so as to prevent business from going over to the railways. This succeeded for a while, worrying railway traffic managers. The worried agent (the manager) of the GIPR in 1868 wrote a harried letter to the Railway Board, suggesting that the railways appoint a person to solicit traffic. Excerpts from his letter are below:

> We are, I regret to say, threatened with a severe competition on the part of the bullock cart drivers from cotton markets in the south-eastern district. The whole of the cotton markets on the south-eastern district are situated at a distance varying from 20 to 120 miles from our station, and the bullock men have combined to charge the same rate to our stations as to Panwell (the latter place is situated at the foot of the ghats on the Bombay river), from whence the cotton is conveyed by boat to Bombay.
>
> The saving by boat to Panwell is some forty pc[50] as compared by rail. I had this week been to the south-eastern for the purpose of seeing what can be done to retain traffic by rail. I shall, I find, have to establish carting agencies same as on the Up district as well as appoint a person specially to solicit traffic and report as to what is being done at the various markets.[51]

---

[50] paise
[51] S.N. Sharma, 'Gateway to the East,' *History of the GIP Railway (1853–1869)* Part I, vol.1 (Second edition), Chief Public Relations Officer,

Eventually, the bullock cart owners' protest died out, just like the strange rumours that had spread when the railways had first arrived. Trains were about speed, volume and faster delivery, and bullock carts were no match. Another battle was won. This was just fifteen years after the first run.

SHAITAN OF THE SCINDE

The 1860s were boom years for British engineers and contractors in India, John Brunton being one of them, with railway mania spreading far and wide. Brunton spent the years 1858 to 1864 building the Scinde Railway, a 173-km-long line from Karachi to Kotri on the Indus.[52] This was the first railway line to be laid in the areas that now comprise Pakistan.[53]

He wrote the story of his life dedicated to his seven grandchildren, in the hope that they would find it interesting and amusing. In his work, titled *John Brunton's Book: Being the Memories of John Brunton, Engineer, from a Manuscript in his Own Hand Written for his Grandchildren and Now Printed,* Brunton recalls an interesting anecdote during the Indian Mutiny that mentions how a mob of

---

Central Railway, Bombay (1990) chap.4, p.89.
[52]Daniel R. Headrick, 'The Railways of India,' *The Tentacles of Progress: Technology Transfer in the Age of Imperialism (1850-1940)*, Oxford University Press, chap.3, p.66
[53]Owais Mughal, *Karachi to Kotri—The First Railways in Pakistan*, September 2009, http://www.irfca.org/articles/karachi-kotri.html

mutineers did not go near the steam locomotive, fearing it to be the devil, and threw stones at it from far away.

> The natives of Scinde had never seen a locomotive engine, they had heard of them as dragging great loads on the lines by some hidden power they could not understand, therefore they feared them, supposing they moved by some diabolical agency, they called them Shaitan (or Satan). During the Mutiny, the mutineers got possession of one of the East Indian Line Stations where stood several engines. They did not dare to approach them but stood a good way off and threw stones at them.[54]

MANAGING WORKFORCE WITH A LUKRI (STICK)

While on the subject of Brunton, an interesting anecdote in his book about railway construction near Bhore Ghat between Bombay and Poona recalls how he had once overheard a conversation between the then Governor of Bombay, Sir Henry Bartle Edward Frere, and a foreman, on the Bhore Ghat Railway incline.

Building the railroad over the Bhore and Thull ghats in western India was a tough challenge. The massive construction for both the lines went on for more than seven years, and about 25,000 people worked at the site at any given time.

---

[54] *John Brunton's Book: Being the Memories of John Brunton, Engineer, From a Manuscript in His Own Hand Written For His Grandchildren and Now First Printed.* Cambridge University Press, 1939

While the workers were native men, women and children, the foremen and supervisors were English. Brunton recalls that the governor and his party on a visit to Bhore Ghat approached a party of workers. Besides a big team of labourers he encountered 'a brawny navvy', as he mentions, an Englishman who appeared to be superintending operations. Sir Frere addressed him in his mild, kind way.[55]

'Well, my good man, you appear to be the manager here.'

'Yes, sir,' was the reply.

'And how are you getting on?'

'Oh, sir, we are getting on well.'

'How many natives you have under your orders?'

'Well, sir, about 500 of 'em all together.'

'Do you speak their language?'

'No sir, I don't.'

'Well, then, how do you manage to let these natives understand what they are to do?'

'Oh, sir, I'll tell you. I tell these chaps three times in good plain English, and if they don't understand that, I take the lukri (the stick) and we get on well.'

The ludicrousness of the whole situation was too much for Sir Frere's gravity and he burst out laughing—and [the Englishmen] were obliged to turn away. They discovered that this navvy was a most kind-hearted

---

[55]Ibid, 'The Navvy's Way,' pp.107–108

fellow, much loved by the natives under his charge, who would do anything for him. He, of course, when he made the confession, had no idea to whom he was speaking.

RAIL CARRIAGES FOR CASTE, CLASS AND THE MASSES

In south India, where the trial runs of the railways and makeshift locomotives had happened way back in the 1830s, the construction of formal passenger railways had now been taken up.

The first Madras Railway Company was established in 1845. After facing many difficulties while getting started, the company was dissolved in 1847. In July 1852 (under a deed of settlement) the Madras Railway Company was formally created in the City of London 'for the purpose of acquiring and holding lands in the East Indies and Great Britain, and making, acquiring and working one or more railway or railways in India' together with all such things as 'might be deemed advisable or desirable for efficiently carrying [the project] into effect'. To this end, the railway company was empowered to enter into contracts with 'Her Majesty's government in this country [Great Britain] or in India, or with the Honourable East India Company' so that 'one or more line or lines of railway' could be constructed and maintained. The company contracted with the Indian government for a 4–5 per cent guaranteed return on the funds needed to construct lines from Madras

(now Chennai) to Vaypura (now Beypore), and from
Madras to the Bombay line. This amounted to a stretch
of 820 miles. Construction began on the first section of the
company's network in 1853. The first train ran along the
completed line from Chennai to Wallajah Road in 1856.
Construction continued and the Madras railway network
expanded significantly.[56] The hot weather of the south called
for certain measures to keep the rail carriages comparatively
cooler. They were made to certain specifications and had
glass windows to keep the compartment cool, and had
leather curtains to distinguish first class from the rest.
There were also fourth class freight trains for the masses.
The following excerpts from the official correspondence
of George Bruce, a British engineer, with an observation
letter written by the consulting engineer, T.T. Pears, gives
an insight.[57]

Madras Railway
Coimbatore, 24 December 1853
Edward Smalley, Esquire, Agent

Sir,
I have the honour to forward to you some drawings
of railway carriages made by Mr Simpson, the coach
builder, Madras.

---

[56]Indian Railway Fans' Club Association website report on Madras
Railway with citations from the material in the Indian Railways Repeals
Proposal–Consultation Paper.
[57]Selections from the records of the Madras government. Report of the
Railway Department for 1854, Madras, no.18. pp.cccxix–cccxxi

I think it desirable that the carriages should not be very large to avoid the difficulty which would be experienced in moving them at the stations if very heavy; this would lead me to prefer four-wheeled carriages to six-wheeled ones.

It would be an advantage to have the steps of the carriages so extended as to enable the guard to move without danger along the train, and to assist in this a hand rail might be placed the whole length of the carriage on each side.

The ventilation of carriages is a matter of great importance; and this will probably be best secured by spaces left in the sides, both below and above, covered with rattan[58] as shown in the drawing, and by venetians to slide up and down, as in a gentleman's ordinary carriage in this country.

On the other hand, to keep out the intense heat and hot winds, the first class carriages should in addition to venetians have glass windows, as at home, and strong leather purdahs to keep off the glare of the sun.

And in addition to this, both first and second class carriages should have a double roof.

In second class carriages, it appears to be sufficient to have venetians without glass, excepting in the upper panel of the doors, where it would be better to have both glass and venetians, and the purdahs could in this case be dispensed with,

---

[58]Palm or cane sticks

excepting over the door.

As the third class carriages will be used only by natives regardless of the heat, the above precautions may be dispensed with, and a carriage having a simple roof supported by iron standards, and protected in some measure by strong leather, or cloth curtains, will be sufficient.

It is probable that the best lining for the first class carriages will be cloth stuffed in the usual way; though whatever is adopted, great care must be taken to keep away insects.

Second class carriages might, with propriety, have rattan seats and backs, and third class wooden seats with a rail for the back.

Besides the provisions which is necessary to make against the heat of the climate, it is also necessary to provide in some measure for the peculiarities of Native society.

It is certainly neither the interest, nor the duty of the Railway Company, to recognize in any way the distinctions of creed and caste, so as to provide one carriage for a Brahmin, and another for a Pariah, and the only distinction made should be that which can be purchased by money.

At the same time, there should be every reasonable provision made to enable natives to be as private as they please.

I refer especially to the case of women, and to enable a man to travel with his wife privately without inconvenience to the public or loss to the Railway Company. I should recommend that many of the first and second class carriages should be made with a coupe at each end.

Then in the case of females travelling alone, it would be easy to assign one particular carriage in a train for women exclusively, when required.

In the above remarks, I have assumed that it will be best to adopt three classes of carriages, as I believe that the interests of the company, and the requirements of the public, will be best answered by such an arrangement.

The plan, originally proposed, of sending out all the iron work (in the first instance at least) from England, and working drawings of the carriages, so that they may be made up in this country, appears to be the best arrangement which could be adopted.

—George B. Bruce
Chief Engineer

As if the details and elaborations were not enough, the consulting engineer wrote back suggesting a fourth class, the cheapest of them all, for the masses, with the goods train.

Observation by the Consulting Engineer
...I consider that arrangements will have to be made, hereafter, for providing the cheapest possible means of transport for a fourth class of passenger with the goods train. Carriage trucks, mail vans

and other special conveyances will have to be constructed hereafter. The whole of the upper works might, with advantage, be made in this country, from the commencement; and I doubt not that men of enterprise and ability will be found in Madras to make, after a little observation, the entire carriages.[59]

—T.T. Pears
Consulting Engineer for Railways
Madras, 21 February 1854

RUGGED JOURNEYS

By the 1880s, the railways had become an integral part of the Indian topography. Lines had been built across major parts of the subcontinent and where the main line did not go, the narrow and metre gauge had taken the lead to spread the railway culture. Such widespread local lines led to large-scale adventures, with some of them documented in history books, travel diaries and autobiographies. The travel diary of geologist Valentine Ball is one such record. His book *Jungle Life of India; or, The Journeys and Journals of an Indian Geologist* (published circa 1880) has notes on experiences of his train journeys as he travelled across the subcontinent.

The finding of coal by Major Sandeman in 1874 near Derajat (today in central Pakistan) required an officer of

---

[59] Selections from the records of the Madras government. Report of the Railway Department for 1854, Madras, no.18

the Geological Survey of India to be sent for inspection. Here is an excerpt from officer Ball's account.

> The climate of the Derajat in July enjoys a somewhat evil reputation, and the Government of India most considerately declined to order any geologist on this mission, but granted permission to whoever might be selected by the Superintendent of the Survey to proceed or not at his own risk. The offer being made to me was gladly accepted, as an opportunity of visiting such remote regions, beyond the British frontier, was not likely to recur, and the trip promised to be one of great interest... I therefore immediately made my preparations, and left Calcutta by train for Multan on the night of the 3rd of July. By travelling straight through, I reached Lahore at noon on the 6th. As the train for Multan does not leave until the evening, on account of the excessive heat by day, I employed the time at my disposal in visiting the city of Lahore and its neighbourhood. I shall not, however, here pause to describe what I saw, but continue the account of my journey. At 5.30 p.m. the train left for Multan. The carriages on this line—very different in construction from those in which I had come through from Calcutta to Lahore with great comfort—were divided into narrow compartments, and heavily cushioned, being apparently cunningly devised to intensify the sufferings of passengers. A slow rate of progression, frequent and long stoppages, and an abundance of flying sand, proved to be causes of further discomfort

and irritation. I, the only European passenger in the train, passed a terrible night, and the natives seemed to suffer almost as much, as at every station the cries for water were unceasing.[60]

BUYING ELEPHANTS FROM EAST INDIA RAILWAY

During one such journey, Ball writes how he was delayed for the purchase of some elephants on behalf of the government, describing them in detail and how they proved to be an excellent investment.

November 16, Calcutta to Assensole – I was delayed at Assensole for some days, arranging for the purchase, on the part of the Government, of two elephants, which were to carry my baggage. Two females, the property of the East Indian Railway Company, were selected; a very fine-looking tusker being rejected on account of the uncertainty of his temper, and the fact that he had killed an old woman who went down to the tank where he was bathing. The two which were purchased were called Anarkalli and Peari, the former a sedate old maid, and the latter a skittish, well-shaped, good-tempered young thing of about thirty-five years of age. Since then both these elephants

---

[60]Valentine Ball, 'Baluchistan and Afghanistan, Agra and Delhi,' *Jungle Life in India or; The Journeys and Journals of an Indian Geologist,* (London, Thomas De La Ru and Company, Bunhill Row, 1880), chap.10, sec.2, pp.437–438.

have travelled some thousands of miles with me, and, except that Peari occasionally suffers from fits, they have proved an excellent investment, and have done their work well.[61]

How the Railways in India Inspired a Jules Verne Classic

The East Indian Railway embraces a line from Calcutta to Delhi, with branches to Raneegunge, the Barrackur river, and the Singharron Valley, and a line from Allahabad to Jubbulpore, where it joins the trans-peninsular line from Bombay. Its whole length is 1,338 miles, being 1,138 miles to Delhi, including branches, and about 200 miles for the Jubbulpore line. The line to Jubbulpore strikes off at Allahabad and forms a junction with the Great Indian Peninsula Railway, thereby connecting Bombay with Calcutta and Delhi.[62]

The above report in the *Railway Intelligence* is one of the key contexts in *Around the World in Eighty Days* (French: *Le tour du monde en quatre-vingts jours*), the classic adventure novel by the French writer Jules Verne, published in 1873.

[61] Valentine Ball, *Jungle Life in India* or *The Journeys and Journals of an Indian Geologist* (Bunhill Row, London, Thomas De La Ru and Company, 1880), chap.7, pp.274-275.
[62] *Railway Intelligence*, (Dec 31, 1870), vol.6

In the story, Phileas Fogg of London and his newly employed French valet Passepartout attempt to circumnavigate the world in eighty days on a £20,000 wager [the approximate equivalent of £2,221,600 in 2018] set by his friends at the Reform Club. It is one of Verne's most acclaimed works. The story starts in London on Tuesday, 1 October 1872.

In 1869–70, the idea of travelling around the world drew popular attention when three geographical breakthroughs occurred: the completion of the First Transcontinental Railroad in America (1869), the linking of the Indian Railways across the subcontinent (1870) and the opening of the Suez Canal (1869).

Here's a reference to the Indian Railways in *Around the World in Eighty Days*:

'In eighty days,' interrupted Phileas Fogg.

'That is true, gentlemen,' added John Sullivan. 'Only eighty days, now that the section between Rothal and Allahabad, on the Great Indian Peninsula Railway, has been opened.[63]

The closing date of the novel, 21 December 1872, was the same date as the last date of its serial

---

[63]Jules Verne, 'In which a conversation takes place which seems likely to cost Phileas Fogg dear,' Geo M. Towle, trans., *Around the World in Eighty Days*, chap.3

publication. As it was being published serially for the first time, some readers believed that the journey was actually taking place—bets were placed, and some railway and ship liner companies lobbied for Verne to appear in the book.

Here is the estimate made by *The Daily Telegraph*:

From London to Suez via Mont Cenis and Brindisi, by rail and steamboats – 7 days

From Suez to Bombay, by steamer – 13 days

From Bombay to Calcutta, by rail – 3 days

From Calcutta to Hong Kong, by steamer – 13 days

From Hong Kong to Yokohama (Japan), by steamer – 6 days

From Yokohama to San Francisco, by steamer – 22 days

From San Francisco to New York, by rail – 7 days

From New York to London, by steamer and rail – 9 days

Total – 80 days

According to an excerpt from *Around the World in Eighty Days*, the general route of the Great Indian Peninsula Railway was:

Leaving Bombay, it passes through Salcette, crossing to the continent opposite Tannah, goes over the chain of the Western Ghauts, runs thence north-east as far as Burhampoor, skirts the nearly independent territory of Bundelcund, ascends to Allahabad, turns thence eastwardly, meeting the Ganges at Benares, then departs from the river a little, and, descending south-eastward by Burdivan and the French town of Chandernagor, has its terminus at Calcutta...[64]

Here is a graphic description of India from the novel:

Through the windows of their carriage the travellers had glimpses of the diversified landscape of Behar, with its mountains clothed in verdure, its fields of barley, wheat and corn, its jungles peopled with green alligators, its neat villages and its still thickly leaved forests. Elephants were bathing in the waters of the sacred river, and groups of Indians, despite the advanced season and chilly air, were performing solemnly their pious ablutions.[65]

---

[64] Jules Verne, 'In which Passepartout is only too glad to get off with the loss of his shoes,' Geo M. Towle, trans., *Around The World in Eighty Days*, chap.10

[65] Ibid, 'In which Phileas Fogg descends the whole length of the beautiful valley of the Ganges without ever thinking of seeing it,' Geo M. Towle, trans., *Around The World in Eighty Days*, chap.14

6

THE INDIAN MUTINY AND THE RAILWAYS

Amidst Mutiny, War and Famine

1857 is remembered as a crucial year in India's history. It was the year of the Indian Mutiny, an uprising against the rule of the East India Company, which functioned as a sovereign power on behalf of the British Crown. Also called the Sepoy Mutiny or India's First War of Independence, it led to widespread chaos and death. There were atrocities committed against civilians by both parties, but in terms of sheer number, the casualties were much higher on the Indian side. India was thereafter administered directly by the British government.

The railways in the country were at a crucial juncture at this point of time. Having been launched four years earlier, the railways as a passenger transport system had more or less established itself by 1857, and its network was being expanded. The Mutiny changed the way things moved ahead. Military considerations had always been important, but after the Mutiny, they took absolute priority.

When the railways were first conceived, there were trade, military and social considerations. In fact, Sir Rowland, the first agent of the East Indian Railway, whose formal proposal for a railway system in India became the cornerstone of British railway policy, had in his report 'Introduction of Railways into India', submitted in 1844, given priority to the need for railway communication in India from a military point of view.

Stephenson had foreseen the economic, military and strategic importance of this new, speedier form of transport for securing the country, where the lurking danger of internal strife and external interference could never be overestimated, given its reputation of rich resources waiting to be exploited. In his famous Railway Minute of 1853 outlining railway policy in India, Lord Dalhousie had also discussed the military importance of the railway system. The truth of Stephenson's and Dalhousie's apprehensions was tested sooner than perhaps they themselves would have imagined—in the 1857 Revolt.[66]

After 1857, lines were built more speedily and strategically, and railway stations were fortified, some resembling forts.

When the Mutiny erupted, the lines in operation were short and confined to the hinterlands of the Calcutta and

---

[66] A. Ramarao, 'Spread of Railways: The Revolt of 1857, Rail Heritage Journal,' http://railwaysofraj.blogspot.in/2010/09/spread-of-railways-revolt-of-1857.html

Bombay ports. The rebellion in Bombay was squashed even before it could start, and most of the action was in Bihar, Uttar Pradesh and Delhi, in areas covered by the East Indian Railway.[67]

DEFENDING A STATION FOR 32 HOURS ON A WATER TANK

An 1858 Mutiny report in *The Illustrated London News* of an incident at a railway station called Barwarie, 23 miles from Allahabad, describes the plight of railway engineers and their families—fourteen people in all—who escaped to the station's water tank and defended themselves for 32 hours from a mob that tried to burn down the tank, threw stones at it and did everything possible to kill the people. Reported by an Allahabad correspondent, it takes us to the scene and narrates to us the intensity of the Mutiny on the ground.

East Indian Railway Water Tank at Barwarie Defended against Mutineers

I send you a sketch of a railway water tank at Barwarie, twenty-three miles from Allahabad. The village in the distance is Barwarie. The dimensions of the tank were about 16 feet high, 22 feet long, 24 feet broad, and depth of tank 4 feet [*sic*].

On Sunday, the 7th June, 1857, at noon, the day

---

[67]Ibid

after the massacre at Allahabad, P.O. Snow, railway engineer, Mr J. Rose, Mr Mathers, Mr Lethbridge, wife and child, Mr J. Keymer, wife and three children, Mr R. Keymer, all employed on the railway, and Major and Mrs Ryves, were assembled at the latter's bungalow at Barwarie, when information was brought that Mr Lancaster, an inspector, had been murdered, a mile off, when trying to join the above party.

Immediately on receiving this news, Mr Ryves and the women and children were assisted up to the top of the tank, we men intending to come down again for provisions, etc.; but, as an immense number of armed natives began to assemble, it was deemed prudent to remain where we were, else we might have been cut off.

The natives commenced to loot, and destroy the furniture, in the small bungalow (shown in the sketch) belonging to the railway contractors, Messrs Morris and Co., which having completed [*sic*], they went in a mass to my bungalow (about 100 yards in front of the tank), where they began to loot everything I was possessed of, even to taking of doors and windows, and breaking to pieces what they could not take away. Having completed this work of destruction, they set fire to the bungalow, outhouses and everything. Then, shouting and yelling, they rushed over and surrounded the tank by hundreds, throwing brickbats and stones at us.

We kept them off with our guns. The top of

the tank had no cover; and the women and children had to be protected by a mattress, which they sat under to prevent being killed by these missiles. The cowardly rascals kept this up constantly (several of us had severe contusions), at the same time demanding money, which we threw to them. When they found we had no more left (having expended 3,000 rupees), they wanted us to come down. We refused to do so.

They then brought straw and other inflammable matter, and piled it round the tank, and set fire to it, which caused a great suffering from the smoke and heat, but, the tank being of brick, it sustained no damage. Finding all their exertions to make us yield had failed, they said they would spare our lives if we all turned Mohamedians.

This, of course, one and all refused to accede to; a party was dispatched, saying they were going to muster a large armed force to escalade our stronghold during the night; we told them we were prepared to sell our lives in protecting the women and children. We were thus exposed (fourteen of us) with no covering from the fearful heat of the sun, very little water to drink, and only parched grain and boiled rice to eat for 32 hours; and had to defend our post against a mob of 3,000.

On the morning of the 8th, Mr Smyth, an inspector, joined our party, very severely wounded, having had to run for his life, accompanied by

Inspector Thomas, who was murdered that morning when on their way to join us. We pulled Mr Smyth up to the top of the tank with ropes. This increased our party to 15. He was too weak from wounds to be of any assistance.

Having succeeded in getting a servant to take a note to the commanding officer at the fort of Allahabad, telling him of our position, a relief of 35 Irregular Cavalry were sent out to us, and arrived at 4 p.m. on the 9th. Glad we were to see them, and a hearty cheer we gave them, inwardly returning thanks to God for this succour, as we should have had to fight hard for our lives that night.

The distress of the poor women and children (without any conveniences) can hardly be supposed except by those who have experienced the heat of an Indian sun in the month of June. Mrs Ryves was killed by its effects. She died in an hour after the relief had arrived, thus adding another victim to the long list of deaths occasioned by this awful rebellion. The villagers, headed by the zemindars, were the people who looted, destroyed, and burnt all the railway gentlemen's bungalows on the line.[68]

—T.J. Rywes
Allahabad Correspondent

---

[68] *The Illustrated London News* (Saturday, Jan 2, 1858) vol.32, no.896, p.5

STATIONS GET FORTIFIED AND PLATFORM TICKETS ARE STARTED

The attack on the railway station at Barwarie and similar incidents during the Mutiny of 1857 led the British to make some key changes in infrastructure. They included defence mechanisms and protection measures in case of attacks, but probably went overboard after a point. The following anecdote about Lucknow and the restrictions on passengers is a key indicator. This anecdote, accompanied by a report, is also one of the earliest documented thoughts on the introduction of platform tickets in the Indian Railways.[69]

With the arrival of the railway in 1862, the symbol, if not the substance, of Britain's industrial revolution, arrived in Lucknow as an auxiliary of the military establishment. In November 1865, Colonel Crommelin, who had served as chief engineer of Oudh under Brigadier Robert Napier, was despatched on special duty to Lucknow to consult with secretaries of the Public Works Departments (PWD) of Oudh and the North-west Provinces, the chief engineer of the branch railway, and the executive engineer of the PWD, Oudh, 'to take into consideration the best measures for the formation of the great military post which is to be made in the south side of Lucknow...

[69] Veena Talwar, 'The City Must Be Safe—Communications,' *The Making of Colonial Lucknow, 1856–1877* (Oldenburg, Princeton University Press, New Jersey, 1984), chap.2, pp.43–46.

to include the Railway Station, Magazine,[70] etc'.

The railway station was located in a vast open garden called the Charbagh, which was contiguous to the cantonment. The site was thought to be commercially central and strategically good, with the cantonments in the rear. The rebellion had prompted the official decision to convert all railway stations. The Lucknow railway station was conceived at the right historical moment to fulfil the decision admirably well. It included a fort, arsenal and barracks, and extra accommodation for the evacuation of Christians in the event of another outbreak in the city.

Its primary function made the railway station a restricted area where only bona fide passengers were allowed onto the platform. To make the city safe it was necessary to erect these intramural barriers between officialdom and the townspeople at large, sometimes with uncomfortable consequences. Ordinary citizens were not allowed to receive or see off friends or relatives who were travelling. Public discontent about these strict regulations was editorialized in the *Akhbar Anjuman*, the Urdu newspaper of the otherwise extremely loyal British Indian Association of Lucknow. Passengers, 'after much pushing and elbowing', would get their turn at the ticket window only to be short-changed or insulted. At some stations, it is customary to prevent

---

[70] A magazine is an ammunition storage place, which was planned beside the station.

travellers from approaching too near [the station] and only when tickets are being distributed are they allowed to go near the station.

In Lucknow, a warning bell was sounded, but this was often so faint that travellers missed the opportunity of buying tickets at all. After the tickets were bought, ticket holders 'were placed in a room and locked', and when the train arrived, they were 'opened out', but the confusion and panic this system created could not be checked. Then, as a further service, railway peons 'order travellers into carriages, and use force if they do not do so quickly, whether there be room for them or not'.

Third class compartments, in which no Europeans travelled, were overcrowded since no reservations were permitted in that class.

The editor suggested that some of the inconvenience to the public would be reduced by, first, permitting general admittance to the platform for the price of one-pice ticket [one pice=$1/_{64}$ of a rupee], which would discourage those who wanted to come to the station out of curiosity, and second, by reprimanding the peons for their rudeness. It was common for 'European ticket collectors...(to) beat or rather kick' the passengers, and those who went to the station to see friends were 'very harshly treated by the police, turned out of the station, beaten and kept in restraint' so that it was very humiliating for 'any respectable Hindustanee to travel by railway'.[71]

THE IRON WEB SPREADS

The Mutiny led the railway planners to lay lines faster and more strategically. The next two decades saw more companies and more lines across the subcontinent. The Sind and Punjab Railway Company expanded northward from Karachi and formed two new lines, the Lahore-Multan line and the Lahore-Delhi line. The Scinde Railway opened its Karachi-Kotri section to the public in 1861, the first in the region that would later become Pakistan. Down south, the Madras Railway was extended to Beypur/Kadalundi (near Calicut) and work began on a north-western branch out of Arakkonam. Further down, the first line projected by the Great Southern of India Railway Company (as the South Indian Railway Company was formerly called) was from Negapatam to Erode through Trichinopoly. The section of this which runs from Negapatam to Trichinopoly fort was constructed in the standard gauge and completed for traffic in 1862, and the line was opened as far as Karur in 1866, and as far as Erode two years later.[72] As lines, locomotives and wagons multiplied, bigger workshops were set up. The legendary

---

[71]Veena Talwar, 'The City Must Be Safe—Communications,' *The Making of Colonial Lucknow, 1856-1877* (Oldenburg, Princeton University Press New Jersey, 1984)

[72] F.R. Hemingway, 'Means of Communication,' Madras District Gazetteers, Trichinopoly, vol. 1, (Government Press: 1907) chap.7, p.183.

Jamalpur Loco Workshop was set up the same year.

The East Indian Railway Company's Delhi-Calcutta route progressed as far as the west bank of the Yamuna, via Mughalsarai and the Sahibganj loop. By 1 August 1864, the first train from Calcutta had reached Delhi. There were through trains running between Delhi and Calcutta. Rail coaches were ferried on boats across the river at Allahabad. Delhi and Calcutta were linked directly by 1866, as the completion of the Yamuna bridge (road and rail) in Delhi allowed trains to reach what later became Delhi Junction.

By 1867, the East Indian Railway extended from Allahabad to Jubbulpore (Jabalpur), and the GIPR's northeast line reached Jubbulpore from Itarsi, linking up with the East Indian Railway track there at Allahabad, and establishing connectivity between Bombay and Calcutta.

Pushed initially by trade and import necessity and later by strategic need, the grip of the iron network over the subcontinent was stronger than ever before.

The mid-1870s saw another disaster in the form of famines, and the Famine Commission, constituted by the government in 1880, insisted on the building of more railway lines, of smaller gauge, wherever major lines could not go. '5,000 miles of lines are urgently needed,' said the Commission Report.[73]

The 1870s ended with the Second Anglo-Afghan War (1878–1880), which led to more strategic planning.

---

[73] J.N. Sahni, 'A Network is Built' and 'Growth of Companies', *Indian Railways—One Hundred Years: 1853-1953* (Ministry of Railways, 1953) chap.2 & 3, pp.14–22

George Robinson, First Marquess of Ripon, more popular as Lord Ripon, took over as Governor General in 1880. He was serious about strategic lines, and pushed for their construction. By the end of 1892, the total route mileage of railways in India was 18,000 miles; and between 1850 and 1892, new railway lines in India were opening up at an average of 430 miles a year.[74] Now that is some speed!

[74] J.N. Sahni, 'A Network is Built' and 'Growth of Companies', *Indian Railways—One Hundred Years: 1853–1953* (Ministry of Railways, 1953) chap.2 & 3, pp.14–22

7

RAIL GAUGE AND GHOSTS
The Little Trains,
a Few with Oxen on Them

The iron web was spreading across the subcontinent at a rapid pace. It is important to note that at this juncture, the railways in India saw the historic introduction of a number of short lines and trains of multiple gauges and dimensions. This is significant from today's point of view, as the Ministry of Railways is on a mission to convert all the existing short lines into the main line. In a few years from now, I fear, there will be no short lines to boast of, except those with tourist interest, listed as heritage, and probably a few very remote ones.

With small trains and short lines, romance and utility went hand in hand. Let's see how it came to be, but before that, let's understand track gauge. It can be complicated for a lay person to understand, but let me try and explain it simply. The beauty is in its simplicity.

If I were to say that imperial Roman war chariots and horses' behinds had something to do with the space between the two rails of a track, I would be ridiculed or ignored.

But there is actually an urban legend that claims there is a connection—unsubstantiated, but very often quoted.

It tells you a story, and, in the process, explains what a gauge is. The standard distance between the two rails of a track—4 feet 8½ inches—is so because the horse tramways that ran prior to the railways had been of the same width. The tramways were built using the same tools as used for horse wagons, and that was how wide the wagon wheels were spaced. Why? Because the old roads in England had ruts that the wheels had to fit into. And these ruts were made by imperial Roman chariots—just wide enough to accommodate the behinds of two war horses hitched to the chariots.

The standard gauge of 4 feet 8½ inches—also called the Stephenson Gauge after George Stephenson, the International Gauge or the Normal Gauge—is the most widely used railway gauge in the world today, with about 55 per cent of railway lines using this.

But let's come back to India. In January 1851, when the question of choosing a gauge for India arose, Lord Dalhousie, who, at thirty-six years of age, had taken over as India's youngest Governor General and was the key promoter of railways in India, selected a gauge of 5 feet 6 inches. Dalhousie wanted a gauge wider than Britain's. It was thought that it would allow more people and wares to be transported, and give stability to the trains. The dimensions had an overall impact on land-acquisition deals and related procedures, and with its quick spread across the subcontinent, this became the standard width of the tracks in India.[75] This is today known as the Indian broad gauge.

A NUMBERS GAME

Initially, trains and railway lines were feared and Indians were sceptical of the railways. But once trains were plying across the country with speed and precision, everyone wanted to take one. The rich maharajas and businessmen wanted to have their own trains and lines. Within a decade of the first run in 1853, the railways in India had caught everyone's attention.

In 1862, Shrimant Maharaja Sir Khanderao II Gaekwad, the Maharaja of Baroda, opened his own railway—an 8-mile network of small trains that ran on tracks just 2 feet 6 inches wide, from Dabhoi to Miyagam. Initially, he did not have locomotives, so he got oxen to run his trains—and surprisingly this proved quite successful. This became India's first narrow gauge railway line.

A decade later, in the early 1870s, Governor General Lord Mayo was impressed with the advantages smaller railways offered, and found them more affordable and viable in smaller townships, where traffic was not too heavy.

---

[75] S.N. Sharma, 'Preparations for the first railway line in Asia,' *History of the GIP Railway (1853–1869)* Part I, vol.1, Second edition (Central Railway, Bombay, 1990), chap.1, p.8

He encouraged a gauge of 3 feet 3 inches, and termed it the metre gauge to encourage use of the metric system.

Soon, rail tracks and trains of different sizes began to crop up in various parts of the country, breaking the uniform national rail gauge and connectivity. This, somehow, had not been expected by the British and was not stated in the original railway blueprint of British India, and led to lengthy debates in the British Parliament.

THE BIG-RAIL-SMALL-RAIL DEBATE

Many were against the small trains and many favoured it. Here are a few arguments that cropped up during the time:

Arguments against Small Trains

A resolution was moved in the House of Commons on Friday, 7 March 1873, that,

> It is contrary to Imperial policy to allow a break of gauge in the Railway communications between the important frontier town of Peshawar and the main railway system of India.

Laing, who moved the resolution, said,

> It was my objective to prevent a misfortune of national magnitude, a break of gauge in the Indian railway system at a point which was most important from a military point of view, and which might be

regarded, in fact, as the Metz of India.[76]

During his viceroyalty, Lord Mayo, one of the most able and popular of the many great Governor Generals of India, became impressed with the great advantages conferred by the railways, and arrived at the conclusion that 10,000 additional miles of railway were urgently needed to supplement the first and main trunk system of 5,000 miles, which had by then been completed. For the execution of such work, with economy of construction being obviously necessary, the Government of India had adopted what was called the metre gauge, of 3 feet 3 inches for the lines of the new system, by which it was estimated that £1,000 per mile would be saved on their cost.

The superior economy of the proposed break of gauge—though advocated by two distinguished officers of Public Works in India—was, however, unanimously disputed by great railway engineers and managers. Mr Hawkshaw, one of the most eminent

---

[76]The reference of Metz, a city in north-east France, has been given in the context of the railways. Despite Metz being a French-speaking city, after the Franco-Prussian War in 1870 and according to the Treaty of Frankfurt of 1871, it was annexed to the German Empire. Metz remained German until the end of World War I, when it became a part of France again. The railway lines from Berlin to Rhine had uniform gauge and the troops and forces were being able to travel and transport supplies between the two cities. But at Metz there was a break in gauge, which led to problems, and in order to surmount it, the Germans constructed a circular railway. Hence a break in gauge was not advisable for India as it could lead to a situation like that of Metz.

engineers in the world, had predicted that the Indian government would have to spend more money in remedying the evil of a break of gauge than they would save by introducing it. That prophecy was confirmed by the experiences of all countries into which a break of gauge had been introduced, and especially by what had happened in our own Great Western Railway.

If one thing more than another contributed to the astounding success of the Germans, it was the fact that they were able to do that which we were about to preclude ourselves from doing in India— namely, to bring up their troops and supplies from the centre of their forces and reserves to the scene of operations. From Berlin to the Rhine, their lines had an unbroken gauge. There was a break of gauge at Metz, and in order to surmount it, the Germans constructed a circular railway.[77]

A subsequent debate ran with a number of members opposing the above resolution.

Arguments for Small Trains

A report on the best width for the proposed narrow gauge railways in India, and their applicability to the Indus Valley by John Fowler, addressed to the Under-Secretary of State for India, dated 25 October 1870, raised some pertinent

---

[77]'Indian Railway Gauge, the debate in the House of Commons,' *Hansard's Parliamentary debates* (London:1873), vol. 214

points in support of the narrower railway gauges.

> I need scarcely remark that the introduction of a
> second gauge in a country which already possesses a
> great length of railway is a step of much responsibility.
> The evils of a break or difference of gauge are well
> known in England, America, Sweden and elsewhere;
> but notwithstanding this, there are many countries
> where the introduction of cheap railways on an
> exceptional gauge has become a necessity, to avoid
> the much greater evil of having no railway at all.
>
> On this question, as applied to the vast continent
> of India, I venture to point out here the danger of
> laying down a general principle. In some districts the
> population is so sparse, the goods for railway transit
> so few, and the probability of much increase so
> remote, that a cheap narrow-gauge system of railways
> may be introduced with financial and local advantage,
> and without any great risk of inconvenience from
> break of gauge; whilst in other districts, with a denser
> population, greater productive power, and considerable
> intercommunication, it would be as undesirable to
> introduce an exceptionable gauge as it would be in
> England, France or Germany.[78]

Fowler simply meant that it was not wise to apply a general
rule for the track. Those who favoured smaller gauges
largely did so from a social viewpoint, to build a faster

---

[78]Accounts and Papers of the House of Commons (Session:
9 February–21 August, 1871) vol.51, p.57

railway with cheaper investment and economic prudence. However, those in favour of a uniform gauge across the country said it was imperative from a military point of view for quick movement of troops in case of mutinies and emergencies.

Nevertheless, small trains and lines flourished. At some places, they were the only links for communication and became crucial for the town's economy. At many other places, they were extensions of the main line.

Below are a few interesting narrations on smaller railways, their growth and their challenges.

BARODA RAILWAY: FROM BULLOCK POWER TO MOTIVE POWER

The Gaekwar's Baroda State Railway (GBSR) was a narrow gauge railway line owned by the princely state of Baroda, which was ruled by the Gaekwar dynasty. The railway track has the distinction of being the first narrow gauge line to be laid in British India, and also the first railway to be owned by any princely state of India. In 1862, Maharaja Khanderao Gaekwad, the Maharaja of Baroda, inaugurated 8 miles (13 km) of a 2 feet 6 inches (762 mm) railway line from Dabhoi to Miyagam.

This was a branch to the Bombay, Baroda, and Central India Railway constructed in a gauge of 2 feet 6 inches, by funds furnished by His Highness, the Gaekwar of Baroda.[79]

---

[79]J.S. Trevor, 'Administration report on Indian State Railways from their commencement to the end of 1879–80,' (Office of the Superintendent of

The existing line of railway on the 2 feett 6 inches gauge between Miyagam (a station on the Bombay, Baroda and Central India Railway) and Dabhoi was originally designed and constructed by Mr A.W. Forde, for His Highness the Gaekwar of Baroda as a light tramway to be worked by bullocks. It was afterwards decided to employ engine power, and three small engines were designed by Mr Forde, and obtained from England, weighing about 6 tons each, with fuel and water loaded. Some carriages and trucks were built in India, and thus equipped, the line was opened to traffic.

The light rails, which weighed only 18 lbs to the yard, were, however, not suited to the weight, and the tyres of the wagons became much grooved. After a short time, moreover, the management of the concern fell into the hands of native officials, who allowed the plant to deteriorate, and the line proved a failure and was closed. The sleepers and a good deal of the woodwork of the bridges were stolen, and some of the rails and fastenings too.

In 1870, a proposal was made, by the consulting engineer for railways, Bombay, to His Highness the Gaekwar to restore the line, and entrust the working to the Bombay, Baroda and Central India Railway Company.

The old rails were sold; the line was re-laid with iron rails, weighing 30 lbs to the yard, on teak sleepers. The bridges were repaired and strengthened, and station buildings, quarters for working staff, etc. were provided on a small scale.

Government Printing, Calcutta, 1881), p.145. Also, personal references from the Western Railway headquarters and archives.

New rolling stock was designed and built by Mr E.B. Carroll, locomotive superintendent, Bombay, Baroda, and Central India Railway, and the three engines were put in order. These were tank engines, cylinders with 8-inch diameters and 16-inch strokes, two pairs of wheels, coupled, 2 feet 4 inches in diameter, wrought iron tyres volute springs, originally costing about ₹7,000 each.

₹1 PER SNAKE TO CLEAR PATH FOR THE MATHERAN HILL RAILWAY

The construction of the Matheran Hill Railway near Mumbai has several interesting anecdotes associated with it. One of them is how the businessman who was building his dream railway offered incentives to overcome workers' superstitions and get the line built faster.

For starters, the Matheran Hill Railway, a tentative UNESCO (United Nations Educational, Scientific and Cultural Organization) World Heritage Site in the category of Mountain Railways of India,[80] is a 2-foot gauge, 21-mile stretch of railway that winds up from Neral at the base (connected to the mainline station) through zigzags, tunnels and deep cuttings, taking the train uphill in about two hours. It was built by an ambitious businessman, Abdul Hussain Adamjee Peerbhoy, financed by his father Sir Adamjee Peerbhoy, at a cost of ₹16 lakh (US$24,000) between 1901 and 1907.

---

[80]UNESCO World Heritage Centre, accessed 1 March 2018, http://whc.unesco.org/en/tentativelists/5919/

The hill station of Matheran had always been popular as a vacation spot, and Sir Peerbhoy had been a regular visitor. He thought of a railway, and building it became the passion of his life. Procuring all necessary government permissions, his plans materialized by 1900 and construction began in 1904. It was a challenging task, right from the digging of the mountain to the building of the line. The curves and zigzags demanded special locomotives and technology. He overcame it all, one by one. Excerpts from the construction diary of the Peerbhoy family:

From 1900, Abdul Hussain Adamjee Peerbhoy stayed with his family at Neral, to make his dream come true. For the next few years, he spent his days and nights in the jungles on the hills. On 20 June 1904, the government declared Notification No. 25 signed by secretary G.A. Anderson stating that the total responsibility of the Matheran Mountain Railway will be upon Abdul Hussain Adamjee Peerbhoy. Thereafter, by Notification No. 34 dated 28 July 1904, Abdul Hussain Adamjee Peerbhoy was authorized to construct and maintain a line of light railway.

When the work on the line started with the support of an Indian engineer (popular as Rao Saheb), a man of mild nature with pleasing manners, there were numerous issues. One of the biggest challenges was that when the rocks on the hillside were blasted for construction, hundreds of snakes slithered out of their age-old homes, and workmen could not kill them due to superstitions. It was only when an offer of ₹1 per snake as an incentive was announced that the workers overcame superstition. Abdul Hussain Adamjee Peerbhoy rode Engine No. 738 on its maiden trip, along with the driver and two attendants, to prove the safety of the railway and the capability of the engine. As the engine reached Matheran, in a surge of joy and excitement, Peerbhoy's coat got stuck in the engine and was torn.

Excited, Peerbhoy showered money on the gathered crowd and workers to celebrate the safe arrival of the train in Matheran. When the news was conveyed to his father Adamjee Peerbhoy K.T., he broke down in tears.[81]

WHEN A HERD OF WILD ELEPHANTS STOPPED THE TRAIN

Small lines and trains were always prone to threats from wildlife. A souvenir published by the Darjeeling Himalayan Railway Company Limited in 1921 documents how herds of elephants stopped the movement of trains and how the jungles near Sukna (13 km from Siliguri), which is now the gateway to the 159 sq km of reserve forest Mahananda Wildlife Sanctuary,[82] were once the haunt of leopards.

---

[81] Ali Akbar Adamjee Peerbhoy, *History of Matheran Mountain Railway*, (Matheran, August 2013), p.7. Self-published by the Peerbhoy family
[82] The Mahananda Wildlife Sanctuary was started as a game sanctuary in 1955. In 1959, it was given the status of a sanctuary, mainly to protect the Indian bison and the Royal Bengal tiger.

Battles of a Popular Narrow Gauge Train

For starters, the Darjeeling Himalayan Railway, or simply the DHR, is known far and wide. Along with the Nilgiri Mountain Railway and the Kalka–Shimla Railway (KSR), it is in the UNESCO heritage list of India's Mountain Railways. With a 2-foot gauge and about 78 km long, the line was built between 1879 and 1881 from New Jalpaiguri to Darjeeling.

Originally called the 'Steam Tramway' and first proposed in 1878 by Franklin Prestage, an agent of Eastern Bengal Railway Company, it was constructed by Gillanders Arbuthnot & Co. The stretch from Siliguri to Kurseong was opened on 23 August 1880, while the official opening of the line up to Darjeeling was on 4 July 1881. This railway faced constant threats and disruptions from wildlife. Here are some excerpts:

> At the ninth mile from Sukna, the track passes through the fine sal and toon forest. Not many years ago a herd of wild elephants disrupted the passage of the train through this forest and the driver had perforce to cut back into Sukna and await the departure of the unwelcome marauders. These lower forests form cover for tigers, leopards, wild buffalo, deer, hogs and wolves, as well as for a host of small animals such as monkeys and wild cats. Rhinoceri are found in the Teesta and other rivers, while the jungle covers are replete with jungle-fowl, woodcock and pigeons of various sorts.

Creepers are seen pendant from the trees, and ferns and bamboo grass cover the banks. Giant bamboos wave their feathery crests above. The view opens out to the south and the wooded plains of the Terai are seen below. The traveller may be surprised to see how rapidly he has already risen from the plains. The railway track now winds in and out of the ravines of the mountain sides with many and swiftly following curves, and soon the first of the devices for easing the gradient is passed (Loop 1).[83]

Continuing the upward journey, fine views are soon obtained over the lower hills. A great wooded mountain, Selim Hill (3,500 feet), looms up in front. The train passes under a bridge, circles round the end of the spur and then crosses the bridge (Loop 2). The spot is well known locally as the haunt of the leopard, and it is said that over a hundred have been killed here during a space of twenty years.[84]

---

[83] A loop line in railway parlance is a branch line which leaves the main line and rejoins it after a short distance. In other words, it is a less important line which leaves a main line and then rejoins it later, continuing in the same direction. A configuration, sometimes known as a balloon loop or horseshoe curve where trains entering it turn through a half circle and return to the start of the loop facing in the opposite direction from which they came, such as the Sutton Loop. The Darjeeling Himalayan Railway has several examples of these in addition to six full zigzags and three complete spirals. (UNESCO listing details: http://whc.unesco.org/en/list/944/)

[84] The Journey to Darjeeling, *Darjeeling and its Mountain Railway* (Darjeeling Himalayan Railway Company Limited, 1921) chap.4, p.25.

Today, many such anecdotes are difficult to imagine and seem out of place, but such stories keep the railway romance alive, taking us back on a nostalgic trail—or rather a track, I should say.

A HAUNTED RAIL TUNNEL

And now here's a spooky tale of a suicidal engineer, his ghost and a sadhu with possible divine powers who guided British engineers to build a rail tunnel, still remembered in his name.

In short, the narrative is about a British railway engineer who committed suicide due to humiliation after he miscalculated the alignment while building a tunnel on the KSR. Deeply hurt after he was fined ₹1 by the British government and unable to face the workers he had made toil for the tunnel, Colonel Barog killed himself with his own gun during a morning walk. The tunnel was later completed with the help of a local saint, who has been acknowledged and applauded in the government records.

For starters, the KSR is a 2-foot-6-inch (762 mm) narrow gauge line documented as UNESCO-listed heritage among the Mountain Railways of India. Opened on Monday, 9 November 1903, the line included 889 long and short bridges and 107 tunnels. All the tunnels were re-numbered in the 1930s, and four that were found unfit for operation were later closed. Thus only 103 tunnels were in operation after 1930. After seventy-six years, in 2006, Tunnel No. 46 near the Solan Brewery was also dismantled, leaving 102 tunnels in operation.

All this tunnel talk is to link the narrative with the mysterious Tunnel 33, or the Barog Tunnel.

The tunnel at Barog (at a distance of about 42 km from Kalka) is 1.14 km long and is the longest tunnel on the KSR section. Trains running at 25 kmph took about 25 minutes to cross it, and Barog station immediately follows it. Barog is a small railway town named after Colonel Barog. When built, it was the second-longest tunnel in the Indian Railways and is still among the longest tunnels in India. Its construction started in July 1900 and was completed in September 1903. It is a straight tunnel and also the longest straight stretch on KSR. Its construction posed numerous engineering challenges as it passed through fissured sandstone rocks.

Originally, a 2-km-long tunnel was planned under the charge of Colonel Barog. Tunneling was started from both ends but due to misalignment, the project had to be abandoned. The government fined him ₹1 and this failure made him so ashamed that he shot himself. Barog station is named after him. The old tunnel and the grave of this great engineer are still there, just a kilometre from the present tunnel. This tunnel was finally constructed under Chief Engineer H.S. Herilngton at a cost of ₹0.84 million. Herlington also faced similar problems in finding proper alignment of the railway track. It is believed that Baba Bhalkhu, a local saint from Jhaja, near Chail, who possessed supernatural engineering skills, helped the British engineers lay this track.

According to the *Simla Gazette*, the viceroy of the British government presented Baba Bhalku with a medal and a turban to show appreciation and respect. The Baba Bhalku Rail Museum was opened to the public by the general manager of the Northern Railway on 7 July 2011 in commemoration of the service provided by Baba Bhalku in guiding engineers for the construction of this line. Many interesting artefacts of the KSR section having heritage value, from delicate vintage crockery to bulky iron bells and weighing machines, are displayed there.[85]

Tunnel No. 33 on the line was given Colonel Barog's name as a mark of respect to him. It is said that the friendly ghost of Barog can still be seen around the abandoned tunnel. At the latest count, there are five legends around it.

The Barog tunnel story gets more mysterious if we go by the legends. We have all heard of tales in which someone dies in a place and then haunts it forever. But besides the story of Colonel Barog's ghost haunting the tunnel, there are four more tales of haunting associated with it.

One is of a werewolf. It is said that the tunnel could not be completed due to animal attacks. Barog, along with a hunting party, set out one night to hunt down the animal but what they found that night was beyond anyone's belief. Barog was the only survivor and described the attacker as half human and half wolf, standing over 7 feet tall on his

[85]Official archival notes from the Heritage Cell, Mechanical Branch, Divisional Railway Manager's Office, Northern Railway, Ambala Cantonment.

legs. He was ridiculed, leading to his suicide.

Another describes the tunnel being haunted by a witch clad in a white saree, who put all those who entered it under her spell; they were never heard of again.

Yet another is that the tunnel is haunted by the ghost of a pregnant woman, who is believed to have been killed by a motorist near the tunnel. She is said to be seen as a woman clad in a black saree, holding a baby.

The final story is about the ghost of a signalman, holding a green light in his hands, luring people inside his cabin. It is said that those who venture in are never seen again![86]

ADDENDUM

Why is there an elephant skull in India's National Rail Museum?

For those who are not in the know, the National Rail Museum at Chanakyapuri, New Delhi, has an indoor exhibit of a large elephant skull placed in a showcase at the centre of one of the rooms. What is this skull doing in India's central rail museum? Here's what the description on the exhibit says:

'[The elephant was] run into by the Up Mail of September 28, 1894 at about half past nine in

---

[86]Vargis Khan, Travel blog, accessed 2 March 2018, http://vargiskhan.com/log/myth-barog-tunnel-shimla/

the night. The accident occurred in the Sardana jungle near Goilkera at a distance of 220 miles from Calcutta. As a result of the collision, the engine and seven vehicles were derailed, whilst the elephant, which was apparently trying to cross the line, was subsequently found dead and considerably mutilated at the bottom of the banks, which is 40 feet high at this point. One of the tusks of the elephant has been preserved at the [East India Company] Board Offices in London whilst the other became the property of the engine driver Mr James Bell.'

8

NEW CENTURY, NEW LIFE
Railway Board, Electrification and a Separate Budget

THE FIRST TWENTY-FIVE YEARS OF THE TWENTIETH CENTURY

The first twenty-five years of the twentieth century proved to be the most important ones for the railways in India. This was the time the railways were passing through a phase of consolidation and systematic improvements, with the government taking over control of small and scattered railway companies, putting a structure in place. In 1900, there were ninety-six different lines open to traffic, administered by thirty-three different companies. Between 1900 and 1914, when World War I broke out, the kilometre span of the Indian Railways increased from

39,833 km to 56,784 km, 1,210 km being added annually.[87]

By the turn of the century, India's railways were being consolidated, with a Railway Board taking shape for overall management of the network. In fact, the process had already begun in 1869, when the government introduced a policy of state construction and ownership, and since then, efforts were on to strengthen this aspect. By 1892, there was a Director General of Railways and by 1897, the post of Secretary to the Government of India in the Public Works Department was created.

BUYING OUT RAILWAY LINES

In the 1870s, the Government of India had worked out a system that was unique in the history of the world's railways. While across the world the trend was either to run either completely privately owned/managed railways or state-owned/managed railways, India became the only state which purchased private rail companies at a premium, and handed them back to the respective companies for management, without any financial stake in it.

> In dealing with the guaranteed companies, the Government of India exercised the option of terminating their contracts in varied manners from 1879 to 1907. The eight major companies whose

---

[87] J.M. Ovasdi, 'Genesis & Growth of Railways,' *Railway Administration and Management* (Deep & Deep Publications, New Delhi, 1990), chap.2, p.33

contracts were terminated during this period were the East India Railway, Eastern Bengal Railway, Sindh, Punjab and Delhi Railway, Oudh and Rohilkhand Railway, South Indian Railway, Great Indian Peninsula Railway, Bombay, Baroda and Central India Railway and Madras Railway.

The companies had been purchased giving fair (or more than fair) price to owners. Before the purchase of these companies, the railways in India were primarily owned and worked by private companies. However, even after the purchase of the big private companies, the Government handed over the management to the companies, who had practically nothing at stake in the successful running of the railways under their charge except their goodwill. The only exceptions were the East Bengal Railway, the Sindh, Punjab and Delhi Railway and the Oudh Rohilkhand Railway, which, after purchase, were put under the Government Agency for running.[88]

THE RAILWAY BOARD TAKES SHAPE

These early years of the new century also saw a formal Railway Board taking shape to better manage and control the railways. The board had full authority to manage the

---

[88] J.M. Ovasdi, 'Evolution and Growth of Control Mechanism,' *Railway Administration and Management* (Deep & Deep Publications, New Delhi, 1990) chap.2, p.49

railway lines on commercial principles. It comprised qualified officers from England trained in railway operations and its workings, giving the organization a professional setup.

In 1901, the Secretary of State for India appointed Sir Thomas Robertson to enquire into and report on the administration and working of the Indian Railways. His recommendations were partially accepted, and on 22 March 1905, the Railway Board was established in place of the Railway Branch of the Public Works Department, the central idea being that there should be a body of practical businessmen entrusted with full authority to manage the railways of India on commercial principles. The Railway Board consisting of a chairman and two members was placed under the Department of Commerce and Industry. The Chairman was given the authority of general control of all matters and the power to act on his own responsibility, subject to the confirmation of the board.[89]

WORLD WAR I AND THE INDIAN RAILWAYS

The Fall of Baghdad

With India making a huge contribution to Britain's war efforts, World War I put immense strain on the railways.

---

[89]Ibid

Railway production, of both locomotives and engines, was diverted to meet the needs of British forces outside India. At the end of the War, the Indian Railways were in a state of total disrepair. Services were downgraded, lines were ripped up to be laid elsewhere and railway workshops had formed the reputation of focussing more on ammunition and military needs than on railway matters.

When war had broken out, the Railway Board had created within itself a special war branch, which absorbed the previously created munitions branch and began dealing with the manufacture of munitions, the construction of military railways and the supply of materials and personnel to military railways in East Africa and Mesopotamia. The 'construction and working of military railways in the East' remained almost exclusively dependent on the Indian Railways system for staff and materials. Figures compiled for 1917–18 indicate that about 1,800 miles of track, 13,000 feet of bridging, 200 engines and more than 6,000 vehicles were sent out of the country. In addition to the extensive strategic use of railways to convey troops and essential military supplies like coal, strategic lines were also swiftly constructed within British India.[90]

A case in point was the army expedition at Basra in Iraq. British commander Lieutenant General Sir Frederick Stanley Maude, rebuilding his army with troops recruited from India, went by sea to Basra. While these troops were being trained, British military engineers built a field railway

---

[90] Ritika Prasad, *Tracks of Change: Railways and Everyday Life in Colonial India* (Cambridge University Press, 2016), p.230

from the coast up to Basra and beyond. The following excerpt indicates how good infrastructure helped the war.

> Oil was vital to Britain for fuelling its most powerful warships, as well as for motor transport. British forces therefore occupied the oil fields near Basra in late 1914. A decision was then made to push up-river towards Baghdad, but this ill-fated expedition was supported by thinly stretched supply lines using river steamers and was cut off, surrounded and ultimately defeated at Kut-al-Amara.
>
> A huge effort was made to support a renewed campaign, with heavy reinforcements from India, by improving the port of Basra, building roads and railways and introducing more and better river steamers. Baghdad fell on 11 March 1917.
>
> There was also a much greater demand on the available locomotives, rolling stock and infrastructure.
>
> The adequacy of transport and supply networks played a major role in shaping strategies for operations throughout World War I and in influencing their success or failure.[91]

This is just one case. Overall, the war led to a serious blow to the railway infrastructure in India on the whole, and it goes without saying that it led to widespread dissatisfaction and public discontent.

Indian public opinion as represented in the Imperial

---

[91]Imperial War Museums, accessed 3 March 2018, https://www.iwm.org.uk/history/transport-and-supply-during-the-first-world-war

Legislative Council unanimously urged repeated resolutions (moved in 1914, 1915, 1917 and 1918) for direct state management of the railways in India, appointing a committee to inquire into the desirability of adopting direct state management. This would have helped the governments of the day to take responsibility and gain larger control, but a policy needed to be in place.

THE RAILWAYS GETS ITS OWN BUDGET

In response to this demand, the government in November 1920 appointed the East India Railway Committee (1920–21), with Sir William Mitchell Acworth as the chairman. The task of the committee was to get into the whole question of railway policies, finances and administrative working. The committee consisted of ten members, and among them, three were Indians.

The agenda was to examine the relative advantages, financial and administrative, of a proper management for Indian Railways, given the special circumstances of the country. It could be directly managed by the state or through a company domiciled in England and with a board sitting in London, or a combination of both. Most people in the sharply divided committee ruled in favour of direct state management, 'going by public sentiment'. The committee also recommended that the Finance Department of the Government of India cease to control the internal finances of the railways and that the railways have a separate budget of its own.

Although the committee report was released in London on 22 August 1921, the Government of India took three years to come to a final decision, and the Railway Budget was separated from the General Budget in 1924–25. The following is an excerpt from the committee report:

> We do not think that the Indian Railways can be modernized, improved, and enlarged, so as to give to India the service of which it is in crying need at the moment, nor that the railways can yield to the Indian public the financial return which they are entitled to, from so valuable a property, until the financial methods are radically reformed. And the essence of this reform is contained in two things: (1) The complete separation of the Railway Budget from the Union Budget, and its reconstruction in a form which frees a great commercial business from the trammels of a system which assumes that the concern goes out of business on each 31st March and recommences de novo on the 1st of April; and (2) The emancipation of the railway management from the control of the Finance Department. The primary function of any such department is to reduce to a minimum expenditure in order to keep at the minimum the corresponding taxation.[92]

This practice continued until 2016, when the Central

[92]Parliamentary Debates, Fourth Session, Twenty-third Parliament. Legislative Council and House of Representatives, vol.227, March 11–April 28, 1931, Government Railways Amendment Bill

government merged the Railway Budget with the Union Budget. The merger of the Railway Budget with the General Budget was based on the recommendations of the committee headed by Shri Bibek Debroy, Member, NITI Aayog, who wrote a paper on 'Dispensing with the Railway Budget' with Shri Kishore Desai.[93] The last Railway Budget was presented on 26 February 2016 by Railway Minister Suresh Prabhakar Prabhu.

ELECTRIC RAILWAYS ARRIVE

Though the process of consolidation of the railways had started in the beginning of the twentieth century, changes were not immediately evident. It took time for the railways to recover from the strain of World War I, and upgradation plans that had been drawn up at the beginning of the century were now slowly seeing the light of day.

Railway electrification was one such project.

The idea to electrify the railway network was proposed as early as 1904, by W.H. White, chief engineer of the then Bombay Presidency government. He proposed the electrification of the two Bombay-based companies, the GIP Railway and the Bombay, Baroda and Central India Railway (BB&CI Railway), now known as Central Railway and Western Railway respectively, and a joint terminus of

---

[93]Note on merger of Rail Budget with Union Budget. Press Information Bureau, Government of India, Ministry of Railways, 16:44 IST. The note quotes Minister of State for Railways Shri Rajen Gohain's written reply to a question in Lok Sabha on Wednesday, 16 November 2016.

both the railways. Both the companies were in favour of electrification, but there were differences on the idea of a joint terminus.

The Government of India appointed C.H. Merz as a consultant to give an opinion. He was the one who had designed the London Underground, the world's first electric railway, in 1890. But the project ran into trouble after Merz resigned before making any concrete suggestions. One of the only suggestions he made was to replace the existing rail bridge on the BB&CI Railway over the Vasai Creek near Bombay with a stronger one. Before his suggestions could be taken up, World War I began, delaying the bridge's reconstruction until the 1920s. By the 1920s, Merz was back, this time as a partner with his own consultancy firm. The project now moved ahead speedily. Plans were drawn up for rolling stock and infrastructure for the Bombay–Poona/Igatpuri/Vasai and the Madras–Tambaram routes. The Secretary of State for India sanctioned it in October 1920. A 1500 Direct Current (DC) power source was adopted for its higher start-up power and easy speed control. The power was to be supplied by Tata for traction purpose, and the GIP Railway also built its in-house power-generating plant at Thakurli near Bombay. All the infrastructure that was required to build an electric railway, except for the power supply, was imported from various companies in England.

India's first electric train ran between Bombay (Victoria Terminus) and Kurla, a distance of 16 km, on Tuesday, 3 February 1925, inaugurated by the Bombay governor,

Sir Leslie Orme Wilson (governor from December 1923–March 1926).

> There had been initial plans to inaugurate the service on 1 January, from Sandhurst Road to Kurla, but it was later postponed to 3 February to complete electrification works and include Victoria Terminus (VT) station. The inaugural function was held on Platform 2 of VT station and Sir and Lady Wilson were received by little Miss Idina Powell, the daughter of Mr Powell, head trial driver from Parel's mechanical department. The line was thrown open after Sir Wilson signalled the power sub-station at Wadi Bunder to throw the conductor wire into the circuit to commence the public service.[94]

Sir Wilson's name was later given to one of the first electric freight locomotives on Indian soil in 1928, classified as EF/1[95] and later as WCG–1. They were built by Swiss Locomotive and Machine Works with electrical equipment by Metropolitan Vickers, England, and were useful on the strenuous Ghat sections. The locomotives have been phased out a long time ago, but one of them, titled Sir Leslie Wilson, is displayed at the National Railway Museum.

---

[94] A.K. Arora, '75 Years of C.R. Electric Suburban Service (1925–2000),' pp.1–9. Seminar on transport technology on the occasion of platinum jubilee of electric traction.

[95] Note: EF1 was India's first electric freight loco, where E and F stood for Electric and Freight respectively which was later reclassified as WCG-1. Here W stands for broad gauge, C for the Direct Current power traction and G for being a goods engine.

The first railway, electrified on a 1,500 volts DC, was powered by Tata and Sons who had set up a hydroelectric plant. The power was delivered from the Tata Mains to sub-stations at Dharavi, Thana and Kalyan at a normal pressure of 22,000 volts. From Dharavi, the supply was transmitted to railway sub stations at Kurla and Wadi Bunder by means of underground cables. The electric coaches (electric multiple units) that had arrived a month before to be run on the line were then the widest in India, with 12 feet width and 68 feet length. Each unit with four coaches, including a motor coach attached with automatic couplers, was capable of running at a speed of 50 miles per hour, smoke-free! The third class coach had ninety-six seats each. They were provided by Cammell Laird and the 1898-founded German train builder Uerdingen Wagonfabrik.[96]

There was no soot, no smoke and no rigorous practices as required for steam locomotives. The era of clean transport had arrived and electrification spread its wings just like the railways had done a few decades ago. India had become the twenty-fourth nation in the world to have an electric railway (and the third one in Asia).

---

[96] A.K. Arora, '75 Years of C.R. Electric Suburban Service (1925–2000),' pp.1–9. Seminar on transport technology on the occasion of platinum jubilee of electric traction.

9

THE ANIMATED RAIL LIFE
Time, Tigers and More Mysteries

This chapter takes a look at the peculiarities that one had to deal with while travelling on trains in India in the first half of the twentieth century—from different time zones to the story of toilets on trains and from tigers arriving at halt stations to divine intervention. The narratives reproduced here depict the social scenes of the Indian Railways.

WHEN THE INDIAN RAILWAYS HAD DIFFERENT TIME ZONES

Simply speaking, the rising and setting of the sun signifies day and night, and when the sun is directly overhead, it is noon. The local time had been set since ancient times based on the sundial. The arrival and expansion of the railway network changed that. Time and speed being vital components of rail travel, the need was felt for a standardized time. The sundial or solar time became increasingly inconvenient as it differed with geographical longitudes, changing for every degree.

As the UK grew into an advanced maritime nation, British mariners kept at least one chronometer on Greenwich Mean Time (GMT) to calculate their longitude from the Greenwich Meridian, which was by convention considered to have 0° longitude, internationally adopted in the International Meridian Conference of 1884.[97]

The GMT was adopted across the island of Great Britain by the Railway Clearing House in 1847, and by almost all railway companies by the following year, from which the term 'railway time' was derived.

So, Calcutta Time was 5 hours, 30 minutes and 21 seconds, and Bombay Time 4 hours and 51 minutes ahead of GMT. Railway companies in India had to contend with different local times, and by the end of the 1860s, the situation had become even more confusing.

In 1870, when the Bombay-Calcutta lines linked up, shortly, to be followed by Bombay-Madras, the Bombay Presidency government suggested that Madras time be taken as standard for the railways. Why Madras? For two simple reasons: the longitude of Madras is roughly midway between those of Calcutta and Bombay, and the observatory there ran

---

[97]Greenwich Mean Time (GMT) is the mean solar time at the Royal Observatory in Greenwich, London. GMT was formerly used as the international civil time standard, now superseded in that function by Coordinated Universal Time (UTC).

the telegraphic service which could be utilized to synchronize station times via the same time-signal system first used in Britain in 1852 to regulate railway time. Madras Time was popularized by its use in Newman's Indian Bradshaw Timetables.[98]

The autonomy enjoyed by Bombay and Calcutta resulted in both retaining local times well into the twentieth century. For the remaining part of the nineteenth century, Madras time continued to be used by all railways. Calcutta kept its own time until 1948 and to a lesser extent Bombay continued to do so unofficially until 1955.[99]

Timekeeping in the railways was by means of standard-issue pendulum clocks at stations and, of course, the station master's iconic watch or timepiece. The clocks at different stations, at least the bigger ones, were generally kept in fair synchronization by telegraphic means—a time signal was sent from the head office or the regional headquarters of a railway at a specified time every day, and the station clock was to be adjusted appropriately. This allowed trains to be run according to published timetables without the confusion of accounting for myriad local times.[100]

[98]Greenwich Mean Time website, retrieved on April 6, 2017, https://greenwichmeantime.com/time-zone/asia/india/time/indian-time-zones/

[99]Indian Railways Fan Club Association, http://www.irfca.org/faq/faq-misc.html

[100]Ibid

WHEN TIGERS VISITED RAIL STATIONS

Three Anecdotes

A Royal Bengal tiger waiting at a station

Though the Assam Bengal Railway did bring about increased settlements in the hills, the area remained thinly populated even till the mid-twentieth century. An old railway hand, who was the station master at Ditokcherra in the 1960s had this tale to relate: 'It was a lonely spot with a tribal village about 5 km away and I could stay there only because I was young and foolish. Trains used to pass at night and we had to wait for them on the platform in order to hand over the lukka (a ringed loop exchanged as a signal). Once, late at night, my assistant was waiting at the platform with the lukka flare when he saw something else waiting beside him. It was a Royal Bengal tiger, perhaps awaiting the arrival of the train!'[101]

'Tiger eating station master on front porch'

Another such account in the legendary Mark Twain's travels in India narrates a tale of a telegraphic message from someone at a station in the jungles of Bengal to the main station at Calcutta of a tiger eating a station manager!

---

[101] Arup Kumar Dutta, *Indian Railways, The Final Frontier: Genesis and Growth of the Nort-east Frontier Railway*, Indian Railways, North-east Frontier Railway (India), 2002

After a while we stopped at a little wooden coop of a station just within the curtain of the sombre jungle, a place with a deep and dense forest of great trees and scrub and vines all about it. The Royal Bengal tiger is in great force there (a remote station in Bengal), and is very bold and unconventional. From this lonely little station, a message once went to the railway manager in Calcutta: 'Tiger eating station master on front porch; telegraph instructions.'[102]

Tigers on the Bombay Railway Line

There's an interesting mention of a tiger attack three years before the rail lines took shape, at Bhandup, injuring passers-by.

9 October 1850—A tiger at Bandoop leaped upon the mail cart and upset it, and the garry-wallah was a little injured.

The mail cart road mentioned is none other than the Agra Road that later became LBS Road, which stands even today.

Another report dated 25 January 1863 states that a tiger was shot and killed by two natives at Mahim, near the railway station.[103]

---

[102] Mark Twain, *Following the Equator—A Journey Around the World*, 1897, chap.55

[103] James Douglas, 'The Wild Beasts of Bombay,' *Glimpses of Old Bombay and Western India with Other Papers* (Sampson Low, Marston and Company, London, 1900), chap.13, p.108

THE DIVINE HOLE OF TALGARIA STATION

A Sacred Sati Spot That Changed Railway Alignment

This is a story of how a hollow ditch at a small station of Talgaria (today's Jharkhand) proved to be a problem for early railway engineers. The 'divine hole', as referred to in records, was once used as a sati site and was a popular place. Crowds of believers visited it even after a railway alignment and the station platform crossed over it and railway engineers kept it the way it was, just covering it with metal plates so as not to hurt the religious sentiments of the people.

The site was the talk of railway engineers and it finds mention in a photograph in a popular British rail journal of the day. *The Railway Magazine*, a monthly British railway periodical published in London since July 1897, carried a photograph of this 'hole', with a British officer in uniform and a local standing overlooking it. The photograph was titled 'A Sutie Relic at an Indian Railway Station—Talgaria Station Platform—Bengal Nagpur Railway', and the details went on to explain:

> In the foreground covered by the iron plates lies the relic of a Sutie. Sutie was a custom whereby Hindu wives allowed themselves to be burnt alive on the funeral pyre of their dead husbands. This spot is a sacred one. Pilgrims visit this relic, indifferent to the railway work that may be taking place.[104]

---

[104]*The Railway Magazine*, (November 1923), p.378

Another reference to it states that it led to labourers working there to frequently fall ill.

> On the Grand Chord line, there lies the station of Talgoria. As the track approaches the platform, it veers sharply to the right, loops around and becomes straight again; there is also an octagonal hole in the centre of the railway platform today. There is a tale behind both the curve of the track and that hole. The track was originally meant to be straight, and indeed was straight before it approached the station of Talgoria. However, when the track began to be laid in Talgoria in the 1930s, the coolies kept falling ill and refused to work. A holy man came and explained what was going on. That was a 'suttee' site, and it would be impossible to lay a track without bypassing that sacred spot, pronounced the holy man. As a result, the track makes a detour, and, as for the octagonal hole, it represents the sacred site.[105]

THE STORY OF TOILETS IN INDIA'S TRAINS

Early Indian trains did not have lavatories. They started being built into the coaches by the 1880s in the first and second classes. The common traveller in the third class did not have it then. By the 1870s, as the railway network spread far and wide in the country and train journeys became

---

[105]Bibek Debroy, 'The 1870s and After: Change and Consolidation,' *Indian Railways: The Weaving of a National Tapestry,* p.145

longer, there was growing noise in the local press and among activists demanding such facilities onboard trains. The usual practice then was for passengers to disembark at stations, but the problem was that third class passengers remained locked inside their compartments until the ticket collector came, sometimes for hours, complicating matters. Many rail companies experimented with water closets, but they didn't work, and rail companies discontinued them, citing danger to health and excessive crowding. The Railways Act of 1890 made it mandatory to provide latrines on compartments reserved for ladies, though it still remained out of reach for third class passengers. It was finally in April 1902 that local governments were asked to ensure that the railways provided lavatories phase-wise in all classes, and by 1908, an estimated 5,364 third class carriages had them, after which it slowly became the norm.[106]

This remains the factual timeline. However, whenever the subject of toilets on trains comes up for discussion, I am reminded of a legend about a letter purportedly written by an irate passenger suffering on account of the premature departure of a train. The letter is claimed to have been written around 1909 (a precise date of 2 July 1909 is also sometimes claimed), addressed to the Transportation Superintendent of the Divisional Office of the East Indian Railway at Sahibganj, West Bengal.

The letter is said to have been discovered in railway

---

[106]Ritika Prasad, 'The Nature of the Beast: An Elementary Logic for Third Class Travel,' *Tracks of Change* (Cambridge University Press, 2015), chap. 1

records in West Bengal, or in the Railway Board's archives in New Delhi. It is very likely that this letter is fictitious (not to mention the terrible language, even if it was reproduced in an official publication).

The letter is on display at the National Rail Museum, New Delhi.

Dear Sir,

I am arrive by passenger train Ahmedpur station and my belly is too much swelling with jackfruit. I am therefore went to privy. Just I doing the nuisance that guard making whistle blow for train to go off and I am running with lotah in one hand and dhoti in the next when I am fall over and expose all my shocking to man and female women on plateform. I am got leaved at Ahmedpur station.

This too much bad, if passenger go to make dung that dam guard not wait train minutes for him. I am therefore pray your honour to make big fine on that guard for public sake. Otherwise I am making big report to papers.[107]

Your faithful servant,
Okhil Chandra Sen

---

[107]Indian Railway Fans Club Association Archives, http://www.irfca. org/faq/faq-misc.html

PASSENGER ENCOUNTERS: BRITISH VERSUS INDIAN

Passengers travelling in different classes of carriage experienced vastly different ambience. Third class passengers, mostly Indians, experienced the worst travel conditions and were adversely affected by the surveillance and regulations exercised by the authorities. Complaints about travel conditions in the lower classes of trains are as old as the introduction of passenger railways in India. Indians who could afford to travel in first class too faced bitter experiences. An amusing yet bitter anecdote captures the tension perfectly.

A distinguished Indian, Sir Ashutosh Mukherjee (1864–1924), a trained lawyer and an educationist, was travelling in a first class coach (as he had every right to do). A British passenger, perhaps a planter or a jute mill manager, boarded the train and reluctantly took the upper berth in Mukherjee's compartment. He did not like sharing the compartment with the sleeping 'native' and, when he saw Mukherjee's sandals, he threw them out of the moving train.

When Mukherjee awoke and saw his sandals gone he guessed what had happened. He then took the sleeping Briton's jacket from its peg and threw it out of the window. The Briton searched for his jacket in the morning. He asked Sir Ashutosh if he knew where it was. The calm reply was: 'Your coat has gone to fetch my slippers.' The train then pulled into a station, others appeared and any confrontation was avoided.[108]

ADDENDUM

Some humour on the East India Railway

Here are a few extracts of humorous incidents related to Indian Railways, collected from *Eastern Railway Magazine*, 1953.[109]

Whose property?

There is a story about an angry passenger who complained to a railway official that he had a cinder in his eye from one of the engines, and it cost him £1 to have it taken out and have his eye seen by a doctor.

The aggrieved passenger asked: 'What are you going to do about it?'

To this the official answered tactfully, after saying that he was sorry to learn of the problem, 'We shall do nothing, sir! We have no further use of the cinder, and from a legal point of view the cinder was not yours. No doubt we could

---

[108] Ian J. Kerr, 'Taking Stock',' *Engines of Change: The Railroads That Made India* (Greenwood Publishing Group, 2007), pp.96–97

[109] Indian Railway Fans' Club Association, compiled by Mrinal Das, http://www.irfca.org/~mrinal/railroadhumor.html

institute proceedings against you for removing our property, but in this case, we shall take no further steps in the matter.'

The train stopped because...

This was a frequent query—'Why has the train stopped?'

Whenever a passenger train stopped outside its scheduled stops, railwaymen went to some pains to give passengers the reason for the delay. There was a case, however, during World War I when a passenger train came to a stop near a junction to allow a war freight to pass through ahead of it, and the guard of the passenger train, who had been sworn to secrecy about the traffic movement, said, 'We have stopped because the signalman up the line has red hair and the engine driver cannot drive past him until he pulls his head in.' He was, needless to say, not believed by the passengers.

The old woman and the driver

This story has been in circulation in the eastern part of India for a pretty long time. The Bankura Damodar Railway (BDR) was infamous for its slow running. It is said that the drivers used to stop trains midway to pick up passengers from villages. One such driver had a regular passenger, an old woman, who used to carry her produce of vegetables daily to a nearby town. Being old, she could never reach the station on time, and the driver used to pick her up en route almost every day. But then the train used to be slow as ever.

One day the driver found the old woman walking along the tracks with a bundle of produce over her head. With the intention to help her, the driver slowed down the train and said, 'Hello, aunty! Come on in.'

The old woman, with her toothless smile, replied, 'My good son! I am in a little hurry today. Let me go on foot.'

10

CRIME AND ROMANCE
A Murder Mystery,
Robbers and Rail Romance

Crime and romance added to the colourful history of the railways in India. This chapter will narrate a few interesting incidents of this nature.

THE SEVEN TYPES OF RAIL ROBBERS IN INDIA

Did you know that there were categories of robbers and criminals on the railways? Well, an interesting work mainly sourced from verbal and documentary information and published in 1909 by Hargrave Lee Adam, a crime writer from the early twentieth century, gives elaborate details about this.

The book is based purely on information from people who have dealt with criminals in the east. The author goes on to write in the first chapter itself that criminals in

India are far better than those in the west. Their greatest vice is, he says, craft, and that a vast amount of crime committed in India is hereditary, with those committing it not realizing many a time that it is an offence. Adam's work categorizes the railway thieves into seven classes and starts by saying, 'There are, in India, as in this country, what may be termed "specialities" in crime, and the railway thief of India, like the coiner in this country, confines his depredations exclusively to that one form of crime.' He further warns: 'The railway thieves of India are among the most astute, secretive, skilful, and difficult to detect of Indian criminals.'[110]

The seven classes are:

(1) The Bhamptas of the Deccan
(2) The Ina Koravars, alias Alagaries, of southern India
(3) The Bharwars of Gonda and Lallatpur
(4) The Mullahs of Muttra
(5) The Bhatrajas or Bhattu Turakas of India
(6) The Takku Woddars or Guntichores of southern India
(7) The railway pickpockets of India

He also added the 'Indian railway servant' to the list, who proved to be a nuisance to the authorities. The methods of most of the railway thieves are very similar, varying only slightly in detail.

---

[110] H.L. Adam, *The Indian Criminal* (London, John Milne, 1909), chap.20 & 21, pp.189–206

The first three classes mentioned are the experts at this kind of crime.

The Bhamptas are the most determined and irreclaimable thieves and pickpockets. They are gregarious, and operate in gangs or combinations. They are good linguists, and they so arrange the use of their different languages that they invariably contrive to adopt a language alien to the district wherein they are pursuing their nefarious calling. Thus, when they are engaged in the Telugu districts, they talk in Mahratti and Canarese; when in Mahratti and Canarese countries they talk in Telugu. They also have a secret code of words and phrases of their own. They rarely resort to any form of violence, relying for success solely upon their skill, subtlety and dexterity.

The Koravars are Sivavites in religion, and wear a horizontal mark of ash on their foreheads as the distinguishing mark of their sect. Their methods are much the same as those of the Bhamptas. They enlist juvenile aid, employing their own or purchased children in the service of their nefarious calling. Having accomplished a theft on a train, they will alight at a station and hide in the latrine until the train has resumed its journey. If they should be thus found and suspected, they will declare they have inadvertently lost the train, express their dismay, and even shed bitter tears.

The Bharwars are a criminal fraternity who engage in picking pockets at bathing-ghauts, fairs, festivals, choultries and railway stations, moving about all over India, often disguised as fakirs.

The Bhatrajas are most unscrupulous in their methods. One one occasion, for instance, a member of a gang helped a Brahmin with his luggage, and then helped himself to one of the bags.

One of the strategic devices adopted by the tribe of Mullahs is for a member of the gang, disguised as a fakir, to sit and smoke in the passenger hall of a railway station. Other members of the gang come up to him, although they put up a show of being strangers to him, and he presents them with a free smoke. This generosity being observed by passengers, they gather round to enjoy the same privilege and end up getting relieved of their portable possessions.

The railway servants themselves also commit thefts and give the authorities a great deal of trouble. Guards, porters and even station masters engage in these thefts, mostly of goods in transit.[111]

DOUBLE MURDER ON THE GIP RAILWAY

The mysterious double murder case on a running train of the GIP Railway in the early 1920s created ripples around the Bombay region. Two people were charged with the double murder of a pay-clerk and a peon working with the GIP Railway company. These men were travelling from

---

[111] H.L. Adam, *The Indian Criminal* (London, John Milne, 1909), chap.20 & 21, pp.189–206

Bombay on the 13 Down passenger train to Jubbulpore, and were in charge of a box containing money in cash and currency notes, to be ferried to an upcountry station. It is best reproduced in an excerpt published in official records.[112]

Two men were put up for trial on a charge of murder at the Criminal Sessions of the Bombay High Court in November 1921 before Mr Justice Marten and a special jury. One of the two accused was a Eurasian named Morris, and the other was a young Englishman named Donnison. Morris was at one time a Baggage Inspector in the Bombay Customs. His duty was to examine and search the baggage of persons arriving by boat and disembarking at the Ballard Pier, to see if they contained any contraband goods. But that was some time ago. At the time of the murders, Morris was apparently without any job and in impecunious circumstances. Donnison, the other accused, also appeared to be a waster without any settled job, although at the time of the murder he was working in a motor garage in Bombay.

The two men were charged with having committed the double murder of a pay-clerk and a peon in the employ of the GIP Railway company.

---

[112] P.B. Vachha, 'Famous judges, lawyers and cases of Bombay: a judicial history of Bombay during the British period,' (N.M. Tripathi Pvt. Ltd., Bombay, 1962), retrieved April 6, 2017. Also published on the official Bombay High Court website, http://bombayhighcourt.nic.in/libweb/ historicalcases/cases/g_i_p__railway_murder_case-1921.html

These men were travelling from Bombay in charge of a box containing money in cash and currency notes, which was being carried by train to an upcountry station. According to the prosecution, while the train was proceeding from Igatpuri, the two accused forced an entry into the compartment in which the pay-clerk and the peon were travelling with the cash box. It was late at night, while the train was in motion, between two stations. According to the prosecution, Morris and Donnison first smashed the head of the poor peon. Gagging him, and tying up his hands and feet, they left him in a pool of blood on the floor of the compartment. They also attacked the pay-clerk and similarly smashed his head by giving him several blows with a wooden club. A jemmy was also used. They then forced open the money box and transferred the money from the box into a canvas bag which they had with them. The box contained ₹36,000 and odd in currency notes and coin. The murderers took all the currency notes amounting to about ₹32,000 and left the rest of the money, about ₹4,000 and odd, it being in coin. They then closed the compartment and went back to their own compartment and travelled on until the train reached Manmad the next morning at about 8 or 9 o'clock.

Meanwhile, early in the morning of the 20th of July 1921, the murder was discovered at a wayside station, Pachora. The railway staff and railway police were immediately informed. They appeared on the scene and the compartment in which the murders were committed with the bodies of the victims was detached; and the train was allowed to proceed. The two murderers alighted at Manmad with the canvas bag; and walking along the railway track, buried the canvas bag in a nullah covered with bushes at some distance from the railway station. They then returned, Morris going to Igatpuri where he was residing, and Donnison came down to Bombay.

It appeared that Morris was fairly well known to the station staff at various stations as also to guards and engine drivers on the line from Igatpuri to Deolali. The railway police made vigorous inquiries at the stations and in the railway quarters at Igatpuri. The inquiries showed that for several days preceding the murders, Morris had been observed loitering along the line, and keeping a watch on the through night trains from Bombay at Deolali, as if on the lookout for something or somebody. His movements prior to the crime had excited the curiosity if not the suspicion of the station staff at Deolali. It appeared that on the fatal night of the 19th of July, Morris, along with another European, had purchased two first class tickets to Manmad, and boarded the train by which the pay-clerk and the peon were travelling. As a result of the investigations made at Deolali, Manmad and Igatpuri, Morris was arrested about the beginning of August, while he was watching a cricket match at Deolali. He was questioned as regards his movements on the night of 19th/20th July. He saw that the game was up; and practically confessed his part in the transaction to the police. He was taken to Manmad, and he pointed out the spot where the money bag and the jemmy were buried. Two days later, on information given by him, Donnison was arrested at his residence at Colaba in Bombay.

Morris was sentenced to death, and he was ultimately hanged. His companion in crime, Donnison, was sentenced to penal servitude for life in view of his youth, and the fact that he had participated in the murders under the dominating influence of Morris, who had planned the whole transaction.

A very striking feature of the case is the sinister role of the notorious number 13 in this bloody business. The train by which the ill-fated clerk and peon travelled on their last journey on earth, was the 13 Down passenger train from Bombay to Jubbulpore; and the number of the carriage, which contained the compartment of death, was 3613. This was noted by Mr Justice Marten in his admirable summing up to the jury. Apart from the last '13' in '3613', the total of the digits (3+6+1+3) also comes to 13. It is such coincidences that keep alive ancient superstitions and give them fresh vitality; and facts, on occasions, are stranger than fiction.[113]

---

[113]P.B. Vachha, 'Famous judges, lawyers and cases of Bombay: a judicial history of Bombay during the British period,' (N.M. Tripathi Pvt. Ltd., Bombay, 1962), retrieved April 6, 2017. Also published on the official

KIPLING'S RAIL ROMANCE

Few know that the famous Rudyard Kipling had a close association with the railways in India. The Wheeler chain of bookstalls at Indian railway stations seen even today was his contribution.

The Indian Railway Library was an enterprise conducted in Allahabad from 1888. It was a publishing venture of A.H. Wheeler & Co., which had the monopoly on bookstall sales in Indian railway stations. It consisted of a series of pamphlets intended to catch the interest of railway passengers, and offer cheap, throwaway reading material. The series began as a result of an initiative by Rudyard Kipling as he sought to assemble funds to return to England from India in 1888: he approached the senior partner of A.H. Wheeler & Co., Émile Moreau, with the proposal to publish his stories in cheap booklet form. Kipling wrote several pieces that mentioned the Indian Railways. A few interesting excerpts of passages from his works are given below.

A Railway Settlement

Jamalpur is the headquarters of the East India Railway. This, in itself, is not a startling statement. The wonder begins with the exploration of Jamalpur, which is a station entirely made by, and devoted to,

Bombay High Court website: http://bombayhighcourt.nic.in/libweb/historicalcases/cases/g_i_p__railway_murder_case-1921.html the use of those untiring servants of the public, the railway folk. They have towns of their own at Toondla and Assensole; a sun-dried sanitarium at Bandikui; and Howrah, Ajmir, Allahabad, Lahore, and Pindi know their colonies. But Jamalpur is unadulteratedly 'Railway', and he who has nothing to do with the EI Railway in some shape or another feels a stranger and an interloper.

[Kipling's work *Kim* was published in 1901. This is a passage describing a train journey. The lama is on a pilgrimage and meets Kim, a beggar boy, who decides to accompany him. This is at the Lahore station.]

Extract from *Kim*, Chapter 2

'This is where the fire-carriages come. One stands behind that hole,' Kim pointed to the ticket office, 'who will give thee a paper to take thee to Umballa.'

'But we go to Benares,' he replied petulantly.

'All one. Benares then. Quick: she comes!'

'Take thou the purse.'

The lama, not so well used to trains as he had pretended, started as the 3.25 a.m. south-bound roared in. The sleepers sprang to life, and the station filled with clamour and shoutings, cries of water and sweetmeat vendors, shouts of native policemen, and shrill yells of women gathering up their baskets, their families, and their husbands.

The lama thinks they are travelling to Benares,

but Kim wants them to stop in Umballa first.

'It is the train—only the te-rain. It will come here. Wait!' Amazed at the lama's immense simplicity (he had handed him a small bag full of rupees), Kim asked and paid for a ticket to Umballa. A sleepy clerk grunted and flung out a ticket to the next station, just six miles distant.

'Nay,' said Kim, scanning it with a grin. 'This may serve for farmers, but I live in the city of Lahore. It was cleverly done, babu. Now give the ticket to Umballa.'

The babu scowled and dealt the proper ticket.[114]

BOAT TRAINS ACROSS THE SUBCONTINENT

Some of the most prestigious trains of the British era ran from Peshawar or Lahore to Mumbai to facilitate the movement of British troops and civilians. Ambitious Punjabis, too, took these trains to reach Mumbai in order to further sail to London to take the civil service examinations.[115]

Bombay to Karachi and Peshawar by Train

British rail historian Paul Atterbury states in his book *Along Lost Lines* (2007) that the idea of running special trains to carry passengers to and from ships and ferries

---

[114]Railway stories from Rudyard Kipling, http://gwydir.demon.co.uk/jo/genealogy/dibblee/kipling.htm

[115] Ajay Banerjee, *Train Tales from a Bygone Era* (Saturday, April 20, 2002), http://www.tribuneindia.com/2002/20020420/windows/main2.htm

dates back to the 1840s. Initially, they served ports on the Thames and the west coast of Scotland. By the 1880s, boat trains were running to ports and harbours all over Britain, serving ferries and ocean liners. The first railways in India were a version of this, but the idea of proper and 'branded' boat trains was based loosely on the lines of a Pullman. (Pullmans were luxury carriages developed by George Pullman that were independently staffed and offered a comfortable night's sleep. The American idea was taken to Britain in the 1870s.) This model was replicated in Bombay in the early 1920s with an elaborate port railway network put in place connected to the main lines of the GIP Railway and the BB&CI Railway.

> Mole station at Ballard Pier was a wharf that not just used to ferry cargo, but also troops and passengers from steamships (built 1910–12, extended 1914 and named after BPT's first chairman J.E. Ballard) to destinations in the north, including Karachi, now in Pakistan. The Punjab Limited train started off on 1 June, 1912 from Ballard Pier Mole station as a 'limited' service on certain days only to Peshawar. The train started originating and terminating at Bombay VT (now Mumbai CST) from 1914. It, however, took several days to get there. Today, it is called the Punjab Mail and takes 36 hours to cover the 1,929 km between Bombay and Ferozepore.[116]

---

[116]Indian Railways Fans' Club Association, accessed 18 July 2012, 11:44 a.m., http://www.irfca.org/~shankie/famoustrains/famtrainpunjmail.htm

The Frontier Mail

Another boat train in the Bombay to Peshawar Frontier Mail made her maiden run from Colaba station on 1 September 1928, but during the winter months of September through December, it used to depart from Ballard Pier Mole station. The Frontier Mail had another reason for its introduction: the BB&CI Railway wanted to give its arch-rival, the GIP Railway, a run for its money. It was the idea of the BB&CI Railway's agent (now called the general manager) Sir Ernest Jackson to run these trains and compete with the GIP Railway. In fact, on the train's return from Peshawar, the Churchgate station building was lit to announce the safe arrival of passengers of the Frontier Mail, starting a new tradition of lighting of public buildings on railways. As the GIP's Punjab Limited took several days to get there, the Frontier Mail was faster and the transit time was reduced to a mere 72 hours. Today, the train runs out of Bombay Central and terminates at Amritsar, in the Punjab, and the name of the train has also been changed from Frontier Mail to Golden Temple Mail. It is interesting to note that when the train left Ballard Pier Mole station, it traversed over the tracks of the Bombay Port Trust Railway, Great Indian Peninsula Railway, and only then eventually crossed onto the metals of the Bombay Baroda and Central India Railway. Ballard Pier Mole station was an ideal hop-on point for the several British ladies and gentlemen arriving from England by steamer. It was also a pick-up point for mail brought in from Europe by the P&O (formerly the Peninsular and Oriental Steam Navigation Company) mail steamer.[117]

---

[117] Rajendra B. Aklekar, *Halt Station India: The Dramatic Tale of the Nation's First Rail Lines* (Rupa Publications, 2015), pp.154–55.

11

NOTES FROM WORLD WAR II

The Assam Line and How Workshops Made Grenades and Tanks

AMERICANS TAKE OVER WITH JEEP LOCOS AND LONGER TRAINS

It is a well-known fact that during World War II, India provided the base for American operations in support of China in its war with Japan as part of the China Burma India (CBI) theatre. The CBI was the US' military designation during the war for the China and South-east Asian or India-Burma (IBT) theatres or war fields. Operational command of the Allied forces (including US forces) in the CBI was officially the responsibility of the Supreme Commanders for South-east Asia or China. However, US forces in practice helped in logistical, material and personnel matters.

Here is a fascinating account of how the lines in Assam were completely overhauled by the American soldiers during the wartime and the scale of operations in the north-east. It is reproduced from the November 1950 issue of Ex-CBI Roundup by Boyd Sinclair.

Running on Time in a Timeless Land

Americans swarmed up and down railways over India, Burma and China; they put Jeeps into service for locomotive power and in north-east India tackled the big job of taking over and running most of the Assam Bengal Railway (ABR).

The Bengal and Assam Railway runs up through Bengal from Calcutta into upper Assam where Assam borders Burma. Across it runs the Brahmaputra river, which roughly parallels it most of the way. The railroad consists of a broad-gauge road north from Calcutta 200 miles to Sirajganj Ghat and Santahar and another 40 miles to Parbatipur. Metre-gauge lines run east from Santahar and Parbatipur to northern Assam; from East Bengal eastward from a Brahmaputra river ferry connection with the Santahar branch and northward from Chittagong to a junction with the main line at Lumding; barge lines on the Brahmaputra; combinations of rail and barge using various trans-shipment points along the river.

Problems: Informal Operations

In India the road was generally thought of as running from upper Assam westward and southward because its main traffic was in that direction—the hauling of tea to market. The war threw this railroad into reverse with the movement of the goods of war to China and Burma from Calcutta's port. The metre-gauge line of Parbatipur was in the main single track, fitted chiefly with rolling stock of the four-wheel type and powered by an assortment of locomotives made in Germany, England, Belgium, France and Czechoslovakia.

The Indian method of operation was friendly and informal—though often protracted. There were schedules, of course, but they were observed in the manner of a timeless land. Although a train might arrive at a station hours late, if the schedule called for a fifteen-minute stop, the full stop was observed, even though loading and unloading might take only two minutes. Efforts were made to step up the efficiency and capability of the railroad.

Improving Efficiency Greatly

On 23 December Major General W.E.R. Covell of SOS gave orders establishing the Military Railway Service. Headquarters were ordered at Gauhati, Assam. Units were assigned to operate the 752 miles of railroad. On 26 February orders were given by Covell that the Military Railway Service would assume operations one minute after midnight on 1 March. When the US railroaders took over, they found the Indians unfamiliar with railroad operation in the western world, and equipment in a bad state of repair. Rolling stock was coupled at times with wire! Indians secured vehicles on flat cars at times with twine of a strength that would make American binder twine appear strong as a log chain!

Communications, dispatching and phone circuits were poor. Most of the line was single-tracked with short sidings. There were bottlenecks, the Amingaon-Pandu ferry near Gauhati being an example. Cars headed one way could not be spotted until those coming across the ferry had gone on their way. There were not enough ferries and tugs to move them.

The Army ordered 10,000 War Department cars, double capacity of the Indian four-wheel 'wagons', which eventually tripled rolling stock capacity. The B&A had 73 locomotives, 401 being metre-gauge, 154 of them US lend-lease engines. By March 1945 there were 442 metre-gauge locomotives, of which 262 were War Department types. Ancient equipment had to be discarded and locomotives borrowed earlier had to be returned to other Indian roads.

Lack of sidings placed a limit on the speed of two-way traffic. Short sidings limited the length of trains. In the first year of operation, 30 sidings east of the Brahmaputra river crossing—the Amnigaon-

Pandu ferry—were lengthened, and 37 more were in process, so that instead of taking an average of 50 cars, they could handle more than 100. West of the river the work was completed—26 lengthened to 4,000 feet each to accommodate 158 cars on the four-wheel car basis. Siding improvement work allowed reduction of block sections from 10 to 4 miles, speeding train movement. Meanwhile, 165 miles of double tracking had been installed.

Two ferry terminals were added to the one original. Seven barges were increased to 12, one tug to three. Tugs were kept on the move instead of being allowed to stand by a ferry barge during loading or unloading. When the Army arrived, not more than 200 cars were moved each way a day across the wide river. In January 1945, the average was approximately 800 a day each way.

Train lengths were increased from 40 cars to an average of 80 and in some cases more than 100. Speeds were increased from 25 miles per hour to an average of 45. The number of passenger trains was more than doubled and the trains were running on time.[118]

---

[118]CBI Order of Battle—Lineages and History, http://www.cbi-history.com/part_vi_ba_railway2.html

HOW RAILWAY WORKSHOPS MADE GRENADES AND ARMOURED CARS

When World War I began, railway workshops were quickly diverted to meet the needs of war and converted into ammunition plants. The workshop administrative office was used as an armoury and they produced everything from hand grenades to 4.5-inch Howitzers and 25-pounder shell forgings.

This is the story of how the stalwarts of the East Indian Railway's Carriage and Wagon shops at Lillooah (Liluah, in Howrah district) did a great job during the war, excerpted from an article by D.K. Whitworth in the *East Indian Railway Magazine*, 1945.[119]

> In the year 1938, long before Dunkirk and Pearl Harbour, the Carriage & Wagon shops at Lillooah had little else of importance to attend to than the maintenance of a steady flow of vehicles for passenger and goods service over the 4,000-mile track of her Railway.
>
> Early each morning, punctual to the hour, workmen's trains would arrive. With the siren at 4.30 in the afternoon, work would cease and the men, perhaps not quite as clean and colourful as before, would troop out and board their respective home-bound trains. A perfectly peaceful everyday routine.

---

[119]Indian Railways Fans' Club Association, http://www.irfca.org/~mrinal/whitworth.html

As the World War broke, the workshop at Liluah, as elsewhere, turned to manufacturing war-time requirements of grenades, tanks and ambulances.

In 1942, India was first faced with the problem of defending her soil from the invader. In Lillooah, volunteers were called upon to form a Defence Unit, and the alacrity with which men responded to the call may only be described as superb. And so, time went by. Military discipline was slowly but effectively drilled into the men.

In the shops both men and machines worked at feverish speed to keep the wheels turning. More wagons were required for supplies. More carriages were urged for troops. And with the passing of days, an ever-increasing demand for even more and more vehicles had to be coped with. No matter what the requirements, whether for the transport of men and material, guns and supplies, Lillooah was always ready to answer the call.

Ambulances and Tanks

Lillooah's wartime activities, however, did not end with her all-out effort to supply adequate railroad means of transport. The building of other vehicular bodies was undertaken, and hundreds upon hundreds of ambulances, water-cars, tanks and lorries passed incessantly out of the gates. Other minor jobs of major wartime importance were heavy orders for 'dahs' and tent pegs. These were accurately complied with and rushed away for service to distant theatres of war.

And so we find Lillooah, untraceable on any map, to have shared not inconsiderably in the defeating of the Axis powers. The trains she built convoyed troops and supplies to almost every part of India; the wagons carried guns, machines and ammunition; the ambulances and water-cars she built did valuable front-line service; and her tanks went into action against the enemy.

MACARTHUR'S—INDIA GETS WAR LOCOMOTIVES FROM THE US

The war gave rise to many unprecedented changes, even in the design of the locomotives that used to run on Indian soil. During the war years of 1939–45, the traditional suppliers of steam locomotives from Britain could not meet the Indian Railways' requirement and the locomotives were ordered in large numbers from North America. These were popularly known as MAWD (MacArthur's War Design), or simply WD (war department) locomotives. The success of this wartime design with strong American features greatly influenced the post-war standard designs on Indian Railways.

These locomotives had bar frames, outside cylinders, alligator-type crossheads, cast bogies for tenders and other prominent American design features. Their satisfactory working influenced the post-war standard designs on Indian Railways.[120]

Named after the famous American World War II General Donald MacArthur, the locomotives had a wheel configuration 2-8-2 (Pony Couple Radial). The MAWD was built in 1942 by the Baldwin Locomotive Works, the premier locomotive builder in the United States. MAWDs were a common sight on the metre gauge lines of the Southern Railway, in the good old days of steam. They were especially suited for shunting duties.

They were not permitted to run at high velocities because their bogie tenders could derail at such speeds; otherwise they were fine locomotives. No railway has publicly expressed gratitude to the United States for supplying locomotives for free. During World War II, the US built thousands of steam locomotives and supplied them to various Allied countries.[121]

[120]R.R. Bhandari, 'Steam in History,' https://www.irfca.org/articles/isrs/isrs082004-steam-history.html

[121]The Indian Steam Locomotive page, http://sundar.altervista.org/Steamain.htm

12

FREEDOM STRUGGLE AND PARTITION

From Gandhi's Critique to the Kakori Train Robbery

India's freedom struggle had its own relationship with the railways. Railway assets were a formidable sign of the empire in the country and discrimination against Indians on trains and railways were always taken up aggressively in the fight against the British. Mahatma Gandhi had been one of the staunchest critics of the travel conditions for the lower classes, and his essay on third class train travel is an inseparable part of the railway history of the era.

THE MAHATMA'S JOURNEYS IN THIRD CLASS COACHES

'Third Class in Indian Railways' by M.K. Gandhi Ranchi, 25 September, 1917:

I have now been in India for over two years and a half after my return from South Africa. Over one quarter of that time I have passed on the Indian trains travelling third class by choice. I have travelled up north as far as Lahore, down south up to Tranquebar, and from Karachi to Calcutta. Having resorted to third class travelling, among other reasons, for the purpose of studying the conditions under which this class of passengers travels, I have naturally made as many critical observations as I could. I have fairly covered the majority of railway systems during this period. Now and then I have entered into correspondence with the management of the different railways about the defects that have come under my notice. But I think that the time has come when I should invite the press and the public to join in a crusade against a grievance which has too long remained unredressed, though much of it is capable of redress without great difficulty.

On the twelfth instant I booked at Bombay for Madras by the mail train and paid 13.9 rupees. It was labelled to carry twenty-two passengers. These could only have seating accommodation. There were no bunks in this carriage whereon passengers could lie with any degree of safety or comfort. There were two nights to be passed in this train before reaching Madras. If not more than twenty-two passengers found their way into my carriage before we reached Poona, it was because the bolder ones kept the others at bay. With the exception of two or three insistent passengers, all had to find their sleep being seated all the time. After reaching Raichur, the pressure became unbearable. The rush of passengers could not be stayed. The fighters among us found the task almost beyond them. The guards or other railway servants came in only to push in more passengers.

A defiant Memon merchant protested against this packing of passengers like sardines. In vain did he say that this was his fifth night on the train. The guard insulted him and referred him to the management at the terminus. There were during this night as many as thirty-five passengers in the carriage during the greater part of it. Some lay on the floor in the midst of dirt and some had to keep standing. A free fight was, at one time, avoided only by the intervention of some of the older passengers who did not want to add to the discomfort by an exhibition of temper.

On the way passengers got for tea tannin water with filthy sugar and a whitish looking liquid mis-called milk which gave this water a muddy appearance. I can vouch for the appearance, but I cite the testimony of the passengers as to the taste.

Not during the whole of the journey was the compartment once swept or cleaned. The result was that every time you walked on the floor or rather cut your way through the passengers seated on the floor, you waded through dirt.

The closet was also not cleaned during the journey and there was no water in the water tank.

Refreshments sold to the passengers were dirty-looking, handed by dirtier hands, coming out of filthy receptacles and weighed in equally unattractive scales. These were previously sampled by millions of flies. I asked some of the passengers who went in for these dainties to give their opinion. Many of them used choice expressions as to the quality but were satisfied to state that they were helpless in the matter; they had to take things as they came.

On reaching the station I found that the gari-wala would not take me unless I paid the fare he wanted. I mildly protested and told him I would pay him the authorized fare. I had to turn passive resister before I could be taken. I simply told him he would have to pull me out of the gari or call the policeman...

Compare the lot of the first class passengers with that of the third class. In the Madras case the first class fare is over five times as much as the third class fare. Does the third class passenger get one-fifth, even one-tenth, of the comforts of his first class fellow? It is but simple justice to claim that some relative proportion be observed between the cost and comfort.

It is a known fact that the third class traffic pays for the ever-increasing luxuries of first and second class travelling. Surely a third class passenger is entitled at least to the bare necessities of life.

In neglecting the third class passengers, the opportunity of giving a splendid education to millions in orderliness, sanitation, decent composite life and cultivation of simple and clean tastes is being lost. Instead of receiving an object lesson in these matters, third class passengers have their sense of decency and cleanliness blunted during their travelling experience.

Among the many suggestions that can be made for dealing with the evil here described, I would respectfully include this: let the people in high places, the Viceroy, the Commander-in-Chief, the Rajas, Maharajas, the Imperial Councillors and others, who generally travel in superior classes, without previous warning, go through the experiences now and then of third class travelling. We would then soon see a remarkable change in the conditions of third class travelling and the uncomplaining millions will get some return for the fares they pay under the expectation of being carried from place to place with ordinary creature comforts.[122]

These were strong words from a strong leader.

The railways in India were also a target of revolutionary groups, protests and arson. One such famous incident shook the foundations of the empire.

A DARING TRAIN DACOITY AT KAKORI

On 9 August 1925, the 8 Down train travelling from Shahjahanpur to Lucknow was approaching the

---

[122] M.K. Gandhi, *Third Class in Indian Railways* (Gandhi Publications League, Bhadrakali, Lahore, circa 1940)

town of Kakori (now in Uttar Pradesh), when one of the revolutionaries from the Hindustan Republican Association (HRA) on board the train pulled the alarm chain, bringing the train to a screeching halt.

The train guard, as a normal practice, got down to find out in which compartment the chain had been pulled and why. Two revolutionaries fell on him and made him lie down on his face. Two others pushed the driver from the engine to the ground and stood guard over him. One revolutionary each stood at the end of the train and both fired shots with their pistols, shouting, 'Travellers, do not be afraid. We are revolutionaries fighting for freedom. Your lives, money and honour are safe. But take care not to peep out of the train.'

Four young men entered the guard's van. They managed to push the box to the ground. It had a strong lock. There was an opening on the top; through which they could drop money bags into it. But nothing could be taken out of it. The revolutionaries started dealing blows with hammers to break it open. Ashfaq was the strongest of the group and ran towards the box. He dealt blow after blow on the opening of the box to widen it.

Suddenly they heard the sound of a train coming from Lucknow. One man said, 'Stop firing. Turn down the pistols. Do not strike the box. Ashfaq, wait a little.' The fast-moving train passed by on the other track. After it had passed away, the slit in the box was widened and the money bags were taken out. During this time, all passengers remained quiet, including the British officers, thinking that a big gang of dacoits had attacked the train. The 'dacoits' walked towards Lucknow with the bundles on their head.

Just ten young men had accomplished this difficult job because of their courage, discipline and patience, leadership and, above all, love for the country. They had written a memorable chapter in the history of India's fight for freedom. These revolutionaries were Ramaprasad Bismil, Rajendra Lahiri, Thakur Roshan Singh, Sachindra Bakshi, Chandrasekhar Azad, Keshab Chakravarty, Banwari Lal, Mukundi Lal, Mammathnath Gupt and Ashfaqulla Khan.

Their aim was to get money for their activities, to get some public attention by creating a positive image of the HRA and to shake the British administration.

Following the incident, the British administration started an intense manhunt and arrested several of the revolutionaries. After an 18-month-long case, Pandit Ram Prasad Bismil, Ashfaqulla Khan, Thakur Roshan Singh and Rajendra Nath Lahiri were sentenced to death under sections 121(A), 120(B), 302 and 396 of the Indian Penal Code. Bismil was hanged at Gorakhpur Jail while Ashfaqulla Khan was hanged at the Faizabad Jail and Thakur Roshan Singh at Naini Allahabad Jail. As a mark of respect, today, the Indian Railways has a railway station by the name of

Pandit Ram Prasad Bismil, 11 km (6.8 miles) from Shahjahanpur.[123]

AZAD HIND FAUJ AND THE RAILWAYS

There is an interesting anecdote of how Subhash Chandra Bose and his Indian National Army used trains during their journeys and how the trains could only run during the night to avoid air attacks from British aircraft. The anecdote narrates how Bose would visit his troops during the halts. B.M.S. Bisht, former general manager, North-east Frontier Railway, wrote a piece in January 2010, first published on the website of the Indian Railway Traffic Service (IRTS) about the war-torn journeys.

The Azad Hind Fauj, or the Indian National Army (INA), used the railways as a means of transport for dispatching their troops in various campaigns in Burma. Major General Shah Nawaz Khan of the INA, who later became the deputy minister of Railways in independent India, writes in *My Memories of INA and Its Netaji* (1946):

> The advance parties of Regimental Headquarters and the two battalions viz. No. 2 and 3 moved to Rangoon by train to Mandalay on 4 and 5 February 1944 but on the way, owing to the railway bridges being blown by enemy aircraft, the men had to

---

[123]N.P. Shankaranarayana Rao, *Ashfaqulla Khan: The Immortal Revolutionary*, Republic Day Feature, Press Information Bureau, Government of India, 2000

cover considerable distances on foot [...] Later the INA troops left for Kalewa in Burma near the Indian border in parties of approximately 300 men and undertook the journey from Mandalay to Yeu in Burma by train and on foot. [...] From Tamu to Humine and Ukhrul in Manipur and then to Kharsom and Kohima on arrival our men hoisted the tricolour on the lofty mountains around Kohima...

The former British intelligence officer Hugh Toye in his well-known classic *The Springing Tiger* (1959) prefaces the departure of the INA troops by rail with an exciting background:

Bose arrived in Rangoon with the key members of his Headquarters and Cabinet on 17 January 1944 and he discussed with the Japanese Commander-in-Chief General Kwabe the coming invasion of India. He saw his national flag planted at Imphal, Kohima, even on the banks of the Brahamputra and the people of India welcoming him with open arms. [...] On 24 January he spent the whole day with the regiment, reviewing, watching it at exercises and parade, talking to his officers.

On 3 February he bade farewell arousing them by his inspiring call: 'Blood is calling. Arise! We have no time to lose. Take up your arms [...] The road to Delhi is the road to freedom (Delhi chalo!).'

The regiment left for the front during the next

three days and Netaji watched their trains move and
he could not withhold his tears...

Trains could ply only by night; consequently, the progress
was slow. Bose would, of course, visit his troops at stations
where the trains halted, to look after their welfare and
progress. The troop trains were bound for Bangkok. Bose
reached Bangkok on 15 May and his troops arranged for
the reception of Indian stragglers (refugees) from Burma
because of the worsening conditions of the war there.[124]

HOW AN ALERT TRAIN DRIVER SAVED GANDHIJI'S LIFE

It is a little known fact that there was a possible conspiracy
to assasinate Gandhiji by derailing a train. Various records
state that there were five to six attempts to assassinate
Mahatma Gandhi since 1934. One of them was eighteen
months before his death, when a train that he was travelling
in was attempted to be derailed. An alert train driver had
stopped it in time, saving Gandhiji's life.

On 29 June 1946, Gandhiji was travelling by train to
Pune from Bombay and there was a huge pile of debris
on the railway track between the Neral and Karjat stations,
with the intention of killing Gandhiji in an accident.
However, the accident was averted because of the alertness

---

[124]Article by former general manager, North-east Frontier Railway, BMS
Bisht, dated 19 January 2010, originally published on the website of the
Indian Railway Traffic Service (IRTS). Now on Indian Railway Fans'
Club Association, https://www.irfca.org/articles/ina_railways.html

of a motorman, M.L. Pareira. Yet, the railway engine was severely damaged. Pyarelal Nayyar, Gandhiji's personal secretary, wrote an article in the 7 July 1946 edition of *Harijan* on this incident. He writes:

> The railway train which carried Mahatma Gandhi collided with the heaps of debris piled up across the railway track on the night of 29 June, when the said special train was in full speed. The said debris were deliberately piled up across the track. The accident was averted only because of the alertness of the engine driver. Otherwise, there would have been damage to the life of Gandhiji and others because of the accident. Since the train was the only one scheduled at that time, it seems likely that the intended target of derailment was Gandhi himself. He was not injured in the accident. At a prayer meeting after the event Gandhi is quoted as saying, 'I have not hurt anybody, nor do I consider anybody to be my enemy. I can't understand why there are so many attempts on my life. Yesterday's attempt on my life has failed. I will not die just yet; I aim to live till the age of 125.'[125]

Sadly, he had only eighteen more months to live.

---

[125] Teesta Setalvad, *Beyond Doubt: A Dossier on Gandhi's Assassination*, Tulika Books, Sep 2, 2015

THIRD CLASS COACH FOR GANDHIJI'S FUNERAL

As in life, so in death. The last journey of the Mahatma was also in a third class rail carriage. Throughout his life, Gandhiji never preferred to travel in any other class other than the common or the third class, and the Asthi Special (the train carrying the urn with his ashes), ferrying the mortal remains for submersion in the holy confluence of rivers at Prayag in Allahabad also comprised five third class carriages.

The urn was placed in the middle carriage, heavily covered in flowers and khadi flags and illuminated by six electric lights, and so clearly visible to spectators from the platform. Large images of the charkha and Ashoka's national lion seal were painted on the carriage.

The train left Delhi at 4 a.m. on 11 February 1948. The urn with Gandhiji's ashes and bones was looked after and guarded during the journey by Abha, Manu, Pyarelal, Dr Sushila Nayyar, Prabhavati Narayan and others who were Gandhiji's daily companions at prayer. The train stopped at eleven stations en route where millions paid their homage. Many sobbed, others wept bitterly. The special train reached Allahabad on 12 February where the urn was placed on a miniature wooden palanquin and placed on a motor truck, and the cortège proceeded for the obsequies among the throng of an estimated 1.5 million mourners.[126]

---

[126] Taylor C. Sherman, William Gould, Sarah Ansari, 'Performing Peace,' *Subjects to Citizens*, Cambridge University Press, p.81, and news reports

THE PARTITION: DEATH TRAINS ON THE SPLIT SUBCONTINENT

The most painful part of the history of the Indian subcontinent is probably the Partition and its related trauma. The Partition of India on 15 August burdened the two new railways into which the old north-western system was divided—the Pakistan NWR and the Indian Eastern Punjab Railway. The situation has been documented in *The Railway Gazette*:

> A programme of special personnel and baggage trains had been arranged to transfer those officials of the old Government of India in Delhi who had elected to serve in Pakistan, to Karachi, the capital of Pakistan, and for several days this programme worked smoothly. Then, however, it was interrupted rudely by the mining, derailment and subsequent attack on one of these specials while passing through eastern Punjab. Though trains were diverted immediately to another route and one or two got through without molestation, the whole situation on both sides of the border by this time had got out of hand, and the movement by rail of the Pakistan government personnel had to be cancelled.
>
> At a later date, some members of this staff and their families were sent, however, from Delhi by the Bombay, Baroda and Central India Railway metre gauge line to Marwar Junction, and thence by the Jodhpur Railway to Hyderabad (Sind), on the

NWR main line, over which they completed the journey to Karachi. This arrangement worked well, for a time, until the disturbances spread to the Delhi area, when this route also became unsafe. As no land route remained available, the remaining 5,000 officials and their families were flown in twenty-five aircraft, chartered from BOAC, operating an intensive shuttle service between Delhi and Karachi.

Attacks on Trains and Fuel Shortage

Meanwhile, communal disturbances in Lahore seriously affected the attendance of railway staff. The immediate effect was the cancellation of trains for want of crews. Communal trouble also spread to rural areas, where trains were stopped and attacked, and men, women and children passengers were murdered. An accomplice of the attackers often travelled in an attacked train and pulled the communication cord at the spot where the ambush was laid. As a result, train crews refused to work trains across the border.

Despite the formation of the military Punjab Boundary Force—since disbanded—whose duties primarily included protection of running trains and station staff on both sides of the boundary, attacks on trains persisted, until finally no train could be run in the boundary area without a military escort.

Eventually, the whole of the Punjab and the surrounding areas became embroiled, and the mass movements of refugees to and from India began.

Many hundreds of railway employees left their posts and fled with their families. To complicate matters further, many officers on both sides of the boundary were new to their jobs; Muslims had moved from India to Pakistan, and Hindus from western Punjab to India. Their lack of local knowledge was in many cases a serious handicap to efficient working.

In the second week of September, the disturbances spread from the Punjab to certain parts of the United Provinces, affecting communication between Delhi and the ports. The GIPR and BB&CI Railway terminated their services to the north-east at Muttra, and the BB&CI Railway metre gauge services in and out of Delhi were suspended.

Even when the country has settled down again, the task ahead of the railways will be very great. Their chief difficulties will be to settle in and train new staff, sort out everything, build up balances of stocks of fuel and other materials, and overtake arrears of maintenance, that have accumulated to an alarming extent.[127]

---

[127] *The Railway Gazette*, (Oct 3, 1947), p.390. Also reproduced on IRFCA website. http://www.irfca.org/docs/history/railway-gazette-partition-1947.html

13

RAIL TALES FROM INDEPENDENT INDIA

Railway Regroupings and the Secret of the Rajdhani

Newly independent India and its railways were a different story as compared to the pre-Partition years. The divided and uprooted railway lines needed consolidation and the first and foremost thing that happened post-Independence (though it had been in the works for quite some time) was the regrouping of the railway system. Prior to Independence, at the last count, there were as many as forty-two independent railway systems in the country, both big and small.[128] Once regrouped, the systems were streamlined and made more efficient. Among the several

---

[128] S.M. Imamul Haque, 'An Analysis of Regrouping of Indian Rlys,' *The Impact of Regrouping on the Efficiency of Indian Railways* (Aligarh Muslim University, 1988), chap.3.

other developments over the years including the merging of private railway companies which were then taken over by the state, I have recalled a select few, not based on merit or importance but stories that are interesting, and sometimes little-known ones, since this is neither a history book nor a detailed story of the Indian Railways.

REGROUPING INDIA'S RAILWAYS

After Independence, it was time for consolidating the country's railway system. To increase the efficiency of the railways, in 1951–52 the Government of India regrouped the entire railway network into six railway zones. Later, from 1955 to 1966, three more zones were added.[129]

The regroupings began with the south zone on 14 April 1951 and ended with the eastern zone on 14 April 1952.[130]

1. **Central Railway**—Came into being on 5 November 1951 by merging:
   (a) The Great Indian Peninsula Railway
   (b) The Nizam's State Railway
   (c) The Dholpur State Railway
   (d) The Scindia State Railway
2. **Eastern Railway**—Came into existence on 14 April 1952 by merging:

---

[129]At present, Indian Railways is divided into eighteen zones, including the Kolkata Metro. The newest zone, South Coast Railway, was formed on 27 February 2019 with Visakhapatnam as its headquarters.
[130]Memorandum of Regrouping, Government of India, p.48

(a) The Sealdah, Howrah, Asansol, Danapure divisions and Dhanbad transportation division of the East India Railway

(b) The Nagpur Railway

3. **Northern Railway**—Came into being on 14 April 1952 by merging:

(a) The East Punjab Railway

(b) The Jodhpur Railway (except Marwar)

(c) The Bikaner Railway

(d) The Lucknow, Moradabad and Allahabad line of the Eastern Railway

(e) The Delhi-Rewari, Fazilka section

4. **North-eastern Railway**—Formed on 14 April 1952 by merging:

(a) The Oudh Tirhut Railway

(b) The Assam Railway (including the Cooch Behar State Railway) and the Katakhal–Laia Bazar and Chaparmukhsil Ghat Railways, which were being operated by the Assam Railway

(c) The Fatehgarh District, i.e., Kanpur, Anwerganj, Achhnera section of the Bombay, Baroda and the Central India Railway

5. **Western Railway**—Formed on 5 November 1951 by merging:

(a) The Bombay, Baroda and Central India Railway

(b) The Saurashtra Railway

(c) The Rajasthan State Railway

(d) The Jaipur State Railway

(e) The South State Railway

6. **Southern Railway**—Formed on 14 April 1951 by merging:
   (a) The Madras and Southern Mahratta Railway
   (b) The South India Railway
   (c) The Mysore State Railway

Soon after the regrouping of six zones, their operation was found inadequate and some new zones were found having a heavy workload. Following expert opinion, they were split up further and three more zones came into being until 1966. These were:

1. **South-eastern Railway**—It was felt that the Eastern Railway had heavy workload and was divided into two zones. The former Bengal-Nagpur Railway was formed on 1 August 1956, into the South-eastern zone and the residual portion of the Eastern Railway into the Eastern zone.

2. **South-central Railway**—The South-central Railway was formed on 2 October 1966 by taking out the Secunderabad and Sholapur divisions from Central Railway and merging them into a separate zone. In August 1967, the Daund-Pune section of the Central Railway was also transferred to this railway. Subsequently, in October 1977, the Sholapur division, excluding the Wadi-Raichur section, was transferred back to the Central Railway.

3. **North-east Frontier Railway**—This was divided into two zones on 15 January 1958 on administrative and strategic considerations. The former Assam

Railway (including the Cooch Behar State Railway) and Katakal-Lalabazar and Champarmukh-Silghat Railways, together with the Tezpur-Bali Para Light Railways formed the North-east Frontier Railway. The residual portion of the old North-eastern Railway was constituted into the North-eastern Railway.[131]

HOW AN ENTIRE TRAIN WITH PASSENGERS VANISHED UNDER THE SEA

One of the most striking events of the 1960s that caused much distress and changed the map of the Southern Railway was the washing away of an entire train as well as the rail alignments in a cyclone down south. Here's the report of the calamity:

Alert—Cyclone Report

On 22.12.64, there was a strong wind blowing at about 1800 hrs onwards from north-east side. The sky was clear. There was no rain and there was no hint of any storm or cyclone which would hit Dhanushkodi in the night… From 10 p.m. onwards, the velocity of the wind increased gradually and still there was no rain. At 11 p.m. onwards, there was a high whistling sound with hissing, and rain began to pour down. Due to the pressure of the wind which had by this time approached cyclonic proportions, waves were bigger and higher and at about midnight, the fourth

[131]Report of the Reforms Committee, Railway Board, 1984, pp.20–21

house to mine collapsed due to water and wind...
Soon several huts began to collapse and people were
running for shelter at the railway station and railway
carriages. By this time, the cyclone was increasing in
its tempo and waves were rising to a height of 40–50
feet and breaking on the land. Though it was dark,
the white foam on the top of the high waves could be
seen and that was how the height of the waves could
be judged. At this time, rain was falling like a sheet
of water and the wind was blowing at cyclonic speeds.
Huts were collapsing and people were running helter
and skelter to save themselves. There was no time to
rescue their belongings as the water was rising high
and practically everything was washed away. There
are three pucca buildings at Dhanushkodi, one with
terraced roof and two with asbestos roofs. Due to
the cyclone, roofings of the asbestos roofed buildings
were blown away... The wind, rain and tidal waves
continued unabated till about 6 a.m. At this time,
wind and rain decreased a little. About 6.30 a.m.,
both wind and rain stopped completely and within
a very short time, cyclone wind [*sic*] began to blow
from south-west with the same intensity but without
rain. Except for a few collapsed huts near the railway
station all other huts were washed away... By about
11 a.m. of the 23rd, I could contact Madras and
inform the fate which had befallen Dhanushkodi.[132]

---

[132]*India Weather Review*, 1964, Annual Summary, Part C, Storms and
Depressions, p.34

Till the time this report was filed on the afternoon of 23 December, the fate of the 653 Pamban–Dhanushkodi passenger train that had left Pamban on the night of 22 December at 11.55 p.m., with more than 110 passengers, was not known. It was only after 48 hours, when the railway headquarters issued a bulletin based on the information given by the Marine Superintendent, Mandapam, that the scale of the tragedy came to light. The six-coach passenger train with the steam engine had been washed away along with the railway line and all its passengers, with no survivors.

The story goes that on 22 December, the metre gauge passenger train left Pamban at 11.55 p.m. with 110 passengers, including a group of school students, on board. The train had almost reached, but a few metres ahead of Dhanushkodi, the signal failed. With pitch darkness all around and no indication of the signal being restored, the driver blew a long whistle and decided to risk it. Minutes after the train started rolling along the sea, a huge wave dashed against it, submerging all the six coaches under water. The death toll was estimated to be somewhere between 115 and 200. The variation in number is because of the many ticketless travellers on board.

The railway line running from Pamban station to Dhanushkodi pier was washed away. When the then Chief Minister of Madras Minjur Kanakasabhapathi Bhaktavatsalam flew over the affected area later in the same week, he said he could barely see the tip of the train's engine that had completely submerged in the sea. Railway officials familiar with the alignment too reiterated the same thing—'Just six inches of the steam engine's smoke stack was all that was visible.'[133]

Fifty years later in 2014, a newspaper managed to track down one of the surviving drivers and this is what he had to say:

> The train had halted at Kambipaadu after a signal failure when I saw the gigantic waves rip the train's engine off the track and drag the bogies into the ocean. I and a few others managed to climb atop a parked goods train and jump into the ocean to rescue a few people. The bogies had been swept into the ocean, but we managed to save a few people who stayed afloat. Even my miraculous escape is an act of God.
>
> —Assistant locomotive pilot K. Nagalingam, who was on the washed-away train.[134]

Along with the train and the railway alignment to Dhanushkodi, a 1¼-mile-long stretch of the historic Pamban rail bridge that linked the Indian mainland to the island of Rameswaram was also badly damaged; 126 of its 145 girders collapsed, though the lift span survived. It was the legendary E. Sreedharan who rebuilt the bridge

---

[133] S.P. Loganathan, '50 years on, Dhanushkodi remembers killer cyclone', *Deccan Chronicle* (December 24, 2014), http://www.deccanchronicle.com/141224/nation-current-affairs/article/50-years-dhanushkodi-remembers-killer-cyclone
[134] Ibid

in a span of 46 days! He was presented the Minister of Railways' Award in 1964 for its completion before the allotted time of six months.

Now officially called the Annai Indira Gandhi bridge, but originally called the Scherzer Rolling Lift bridge (because it was a cantilever bridge) after its American-born designer engineer William Scherzer, or simply the Pamban bridge, it was first built in 1914 by the British for smoother administrative control by bringing provinces, towns, districts and villages in Rameswaram in contact with mainland Tamil Nadu.

SECRETS OF INDIA'S FIRST RAJDHANI

Rajdhani Express passenger trains were first introduced in the late 1960s. Other trains until then used to run at a maximum speed of 100 kmph and the brief to run the fully air-conditioned train was to take the speed up to 120 kmph. It had a whole lot of critics and there was 'objection after objection' including from the then Railway Board chairman himself.[135] Doubts came from all quarters, including the Parliament.

Ashutosh K. Banerji, part of the select group at the Railways' Research, Designs and Standards Organization

---

[135] *Financial Express,* Nov 21, 2017, http://www.financialexpress.com/india-news/piyush-goyals-cool-reply-to-bullet-train-critics-rajdhani-the-last-new-technology-introduced-in-railways/941730/Piyush Goyal's cool reply to bullet train critics: Rajdhani has the last new technology introduced in railways!

(RDSO), which conceived and operationalized the Rajdhani, told me there were many objections but they were met with practical solutions. This is what Banerji, now 80, remembered and penned down promptly when I asked him to recollect the circumstances, the objections and the conditions under which the then fastest train—the Rajdhani Express—was allowed to run:

Objections

1. The Rajdhani would affect train operations, particularly that of freight trains, as it would need the same space required for three trains in front of it on the same track, given its speed. The steep speed differential between the Rajdhani and other trains would have to be taken into account. This would have an adverse effect on line capacity.

2. It would not be commensurate with the government's policy of ushering in a socialistic pattern of society. It would be an elite service catering to the upper crust of society.

3. Air-conditioned travel in 1969 was considered a luxury. At that time somehow transporting the teeming millions was the primary objective.

4. Passenger comfort and amenities were not a priority area at that time. Movement of freight was. (India was then a growing nation with a number of industries being set up at that time, and railway freight was as important as passenger trains. The Rajdhani, at that time, was probably a fancy idea.)

5. The existing infrastructure, especially the railway tracks, and signalling, would not be able to support increased speeds. A massive upgrade of infrastructure with a stronger track structure and more reliable signalling needing substantial investments were required before increase in speed beyond the prevailing 100 kmph could be contemplated.

6. A committee of directors would need to identify the infrastructural upgrades required.

7. Premature increase of speed before these upgrades were put in place would be a misadventure, leading to accidents and other safety concerns.[136]

Responses

1. Two years of detailed instrumented field trials by the RDSO team had established that our bridges and signalling systems were capable of permitting higher speeds with WDM4 class diesel-electric locomotives and Integral Coach Factory (ICF) all coil bogies.

2. Improved system of maintenance based upon track geometry would compensate for deficiencies in track structure.

3. Improvement in the braking system and the provision of additional distant signals would take care of the signalling deficiencies.

4. Periodic track monitoring by oscillograph cars and track recording cars would ensure consistency in track geometry round the year.

---

[136]Personal correspondence

5. Need for capital investments was obviated through human efforts. This was a significant departure in approach from the rest of the world.

Banerji recollects, 'The proof of the pudding is in eating it. We ran a shadow express for six months after the technical trials, and studies were successfully completed. This established the operational feasibility of increasing speeds. The prophets of doom were proved wrong. We were mad, motivated and bursting with passion to implement the introduction of the Rajdhani Express. We convinced the government that it was not an elitist idea but a poor man's high speed dream train. Finally, our madness and passion won the day. This is what I can recall.'[137]

Such is the fascinating story of the first fully air-conditioned Rajdhani Express between New Delhi and Howrah, which was introduced on 1 March 1969 at a speed of 120 kmph without any additional investment, except for the cost of the train and its coaches.

---

[137]Personal correspondence

14

TRAINS OF PROGRESS AND POLITICS

From Dramatic Sackings to Building Engineeing Marvels

RAIL BOARD CHIEF WHO WAS SACKED WHILE ON THE TRAIN

Bankim Chandra Ganguli, a visionary, strict disciplinarian and no-nonsense officer, was one of the idols of railway icon E. Sreedharan. It was Ganguli who, as general manager of Southern Railway, called upon Sreedharan and advanced the six-month deadline of the restoration of the Pamban bridge to three months. Sreedharan, who had immense respect for Ganguli, did not say no out of respect and completed the project much earlier.

But sadly, Ganguli's case turned out to be gloomy in the Indian Railways' history due to his dramatic dismissal by the Railway Minister in the 1970s. Rarely has a top government official been given the boot in as bizarre a fashion as he was. The incident has been described in *Time* magazine in detail.

> This was in 1971. There had been differences between Railway Minister Kengal Hanumanthaiya, 63, a Karnataka politician, and Ganguli, who was then the Railway Board Chairman. As time went by, the differences widened. On 8 October 1971, Ganguli, who had scheduled a nine-day inspection tour of Gujarat, had just got in, along with his wife and personal staff, in his air-conditioned inspection saloon coach at Sarai Rohilla attached to a train that was to leave.
>
> The station officials received a communication from the minister's office, getting the coach detached minutes before the train's departure. An angry Ganguli called for a press conference on the station platform and stayed in the coach in protest for six days. On 12 October 1971, the government issued an order to forcibly retire Ganguli, and officials tucked it to the side of the coach in which he was protesting. It was sad to see how an outstanding officer of merit with thirty-four years of glorious service was dismissed overnight. It left the nation and the country's bureaucracy in shock.[138]

---

[138]'Shunted Aside,' *Time Magazine* (Monday, 25 October 1971), http://content.time.com/time/magazine/article/0,9171,877315,00.html

'MONDAY AFTERNOON MASSACRE' AT RAIL BHAVAN

This story is about a head-on collision, not with trains, but between the Railway Minister and the Railway Board Chief. The then Railway Minister A.B.A. Ghani Khan Choudhury (Railway Minister from 2 September 1982 to 31 December 1984) was at constant loggerheads with the Railway Board Chief, Mohinder Singh Gujral, an officer of the Indian Railway Traffic Service. Gujral, a no-nonsense tough officer, had been a star, and overturned the fortunes of the railways in his short stint. He had been personally picked by Prime Minister Indira Gandhi to steer the sinking ship of the Indian Railways two years earlier in 1980, catapulted to the post of Chairman, Railway Board and Member Traffic, and Principal Secretary, Ministry of Railways, with an extension in service beyond superannuation.[139]

Choudhury was a temperamental man, and when his appointment as Railway Minister was announced in September, many railway officials saw red. But Gujral went ahead full steam with the same drive that had helped him bring about a dramatic improvement in railway performance since he took charge in November 1980. Choudhury was soon issuing a series of orders that the officials frequently

---

[139]M.S. Gujral, 'Architect of Indian Railways' Great Turnaround,' *Avani, The Earth*, Journal of the Indian Railways Institute of Transport Management (July–September 2012), pp.7–8, http://www.iritm. indianrailways.gov.in/uploads/files/1345724978346-Newsletter-July%202012-Final.pdf

found impossible to carry out, and the minister responded by roundly condemning the railways at internal meetings and elsewhere. The atmosphere was quickly charged with tension as acid file notings went back and forth. 'Don't treat me like a child,' Choudhury is reported to have once told Gujral.[140] The tensions escalated and Choudhury shunted Gujral into retirement.

This is an example of how powerful governments can be. No civil servant has won a battle with a minister. And given the open war between Railway Minister A.B.A. Ghani Khan Choudhury and Railway Board Chairman Mohinder Singh Gujral, it was only a matter of time before Gujral finally went as he did in what railwaymen are beginning to call the 'Monday afternoon massacre'.

Shunted into retirement, siding along with Gujral was his fellow board member and someone who might have been his successor, B.B. Lal. With a third member of the five-man board due to retire by the month-end, and a fourth having been changed just a month earlier, Choudhury had achieved the clean sweep he had threatened during his now famous press conference the previous December.

The broom reached one rung lower: about a dozen heads of departments in the Railway Board were simultaneously transferred to the most out-of-the-way stations. Many of them had been Gujral's most trusted aides and closest colleagues, hand-picked by him for key slots.

---

[140]https://www.indiatoday.in/magazine/economy/story/19830115-railway-minister-ghani-khan-choudhury-threatens-dismissal-of-railway-board-chairman-770358-2013-07-26

In dismissing Gujral and Lal, Choudhury had made use of the prime minister's January directive to dispense with the service of superannuated officers: both Gujral and Lal were on extension. But Gujral's sacking was clearly not what Mrs Gandhi had intended.

As early as last December, Choudhury had sent a proposal to replace Gujral with Lal, and failed to get clearance from the Cabinet's Appointments Committee. Now, using a handle conveniently within his reach, Choudhury had clearly upstaged Mrs Gandhi and presented her with a fait accompli.

The dismissals and transfers were carried out with a vengeance, and with all the drama of a coup d'etat. Gujral, on tour in Bombay, was informed of his dismissal over the telephone. Lal was served with a cheque for three months' salary in lieu of notice, and promptly left his office.

The name plates of these and other officers were removed with indecent haste, their rooms immediately locked; in some cases, sealed cupboards were shifted to other offices. The transferred officers were asked to report at their new posts in two days—often at locations two days' train journeys away. Many of them, in their new postings, would have to report to officers junior to them in the service hierarchy.

Gujral took his dismissal philosophically, seeing himself as the vanquished hero going down in a blaze of glory. 'I have no regrets. I have had more than a full innings, and taken the railways to the pinnacle of their performance.'[141]

---

[141]http://indiatoday.intoday.in/story/railway-minister-ghani-

SURVEY OF INDIA'S 'EXTREME RAILWAY' ON BIKES

This is the fascinating story of the beginnings of India's 'Extreme Railway', as British TV presenter Chris Tarrant calls the 760-km Konkan Railway. This narrative is about how railway pioneers built offices in a week and how survey engineers on Kawasaki bikes decided on the rail alignment to kick off work.[142]

Office within a Week

Within days of the corporation being set up, the team already felt like a well-knit family that had a job to do, quickly. There was no time to waste and the managing director of Konkan Railways, Mr E. Sreedharan, brought home the message forcefully. Three days after B. Rajaram arrived in the city he received a call from Mr Sreedharan. 'I'm coming in two days,' Mr Sreedharan told him. 'I want to see the alignments.' Mr Rajaram at that point had nothing more than ₹5 lakh and a briefcase. He knew few people in Panaji and had no fixed address. Yet, these factors were by no means going to be allowed to hinder progress. 'It was the finest example of how Mr Sreedharan worked.'

Meeting the challenge head-on, Mr Rajaram went to Vasco, hired khalasis,[143] tore up a piece of red cloth to make

---

khan-choudhury-sacks-railway-board-chairman-mohinder-singh-gujral/1/372312.html

[142]Menka Shivdasani and Raju Kane, 'The Beginnings', *Konkan Railway—A Dream Come True,* (KRCL, 1998), chap.20–21

[143]Khalasis are railway gangmen.

'flags', found some stones and set to work, charting out the alignment. By the time Mr Sreedharan arrived, Mr Rajaram had decided on eight locations and three river crossings.

By this time, Mr Rajaram also succeeded in setting up an office—a flat provided to him by Carmo Gracias, an acquaintance he had met a couple of days earlier for the first time at a party—and furnished it by purchasing furniture from Godrej.

It just happened that the furniture was readily available at that point because the Goa government had ordered it. But when Mr Rajaram produced his cheque book and said he would pay at once, Godrej had no choice but to give it to him instead. This was a most unusual way indeed for the railways to work!

'Godrej could not believe that someone from the railways was functioning in this manner,' smiles Mr Rajaram.

'Then they got excited.' Mr Rajaram's behaviour was all the more astonishing because he then said, pointing to a typist in the office, 'I want that typewriter. And—what's that girl's name? I want the girl too!'

By 10.30 a.m. the next day, minutes before Mr Sreedharan arrived, there was a fully functional office, and the beginnings of the alignment in Goa. The typewriter was there too, and so was the typist. Little details, like making a rubber stamp, had been taken care of as well. Mr Rajaram had been in Goa for less than a week.

These were the humble beginnings of the Konkan Railways.

The then Railway Minister George Fernandes had

announced in Parliament that the whole project would be completed in five years' time, and Rajaram and his team did not waste a day on the ground. With such a tight deadline, engineers had to think fast, and creatively. 'Conventionally,' says Mr Rajaram, 'when an alignment needs to be worked out, you require several Jeeps, and lots of people running around.' Mr Rajaram thought there were better ways. What he did was take satellite images, make topographical maps with high accuracy, and send out teams on motorcycles.

He ordered several Kawasaki bikes, modified to carry equipment like levelling instruments, and hired young boys, fresh with engineering diplomas, to go around the state. They were given ₹100 per day, and petrol, neither of which they had to account for. 'They had the freedom to go off to the beach and have a good time, so long as they produced a certain amount of work every day,' says Mr Rajaram. 'Of course,' he adds, with a slight smile, 'the targets they were set meant they would have to work fourteen hours a day. But they felt empowered, and so they gave their best. It helped that despite their inexperience, they were given the designation of "engineer", a title they could flaunt with pride.'

Thirty such teams in Goa worked on sixteen alignments, and the data was analysed, often way past midnight, on an assembled computer that Mr Rajaram had bought cheap in Bangalore (now Bengaluru). Mr Rajaram, who is a technical wizard, designed the software for this analysis himself.[144]

---

[144]Personal interview with B. Rajaram, detailing this aspect

'MILKMAN' RAIL MINISTER AND A FARE CUT

Soon after the railways had earned a cash surplus of ₹15,000 crore (US$3.5 billion) in 2006, Railway Minister Lalu Prasad Yadav was keen for this financial gain to translate into rewards for railway employees, and tangible benefits for the poor travellers who relied on the railways for transportation.

Of his propositions, the most striking was his insistence on reducing second class passenger fares by a rupee per passenger. The Railway Board members were perplexed. Why reduce just one rupee? In most transactions nowadays, a rupee has no value. This fare reduction would have cost the railways ₹250 crore (US$58 million) and the passengers would hardly benefit. The Minister responded in typical colloquial fashion:

Hathua ki gwalan apna Dilli me nahi balki Siwan me bechati hai. Aur Hathua se Siwan ka kiraya maatr Saat rupaih hai.

(A milk vendor from Hathua—the minister's area in Bihar in eastern India—sells her milk not in Delhi, but in Siwan. And the train fare from Hathua to Siwan is just ₹7.)

Lagta hai ki air-conditioned office me rahne walon ko yeh ehsaas nahi hota ki ek garib gwalan ke liye ek rupaih ke kya kimat hoti hai.

(It seems that those who reside in air-conditioned offices do not realize what a rupee means to a poor milk vendor.)

Further, the minister elaborated that it was likely that all the vendor's relatives lived within a 70-mile radius, and thus most of her work- and life-related train trips were within this small radius.

This argument was persuasive and at the end of this exchange, the Railway Board agreed to a ₹1 fare reduction.[145]

---

[145] Shagun Mehrotra and Sudhir Kumar, 'Bankruptcy to Billions,' *Bankruptcy to Billions: How the Indian Railways Transformed* (Oxford University Press, 2009), p.1

15

OF METROS AND HIGH SPEED RAIL
The New Millennium and
Future Rail Cities

END OF THE BRITISH RAIL ERA IN 2013

In 2012, as part of the process to phase out several old pieces of legislation considered as 'being spent, obsolete, unnecessary or otherwise not now of practical utility', the British Parliament put up for scrapping thirty-eight old British-era Acts that no longer remained in force. Among them was the Great Indian Peninsula Railway Act of 1949 that laid the foundations of India's earliest railway company. It was the passing of this Act in the British Parliament in 1849 that had led to the establishment of the rail company that ran India's first train.[146]

---

[146]Statute Law Repeals: Twentieth Report Draft Statute Law (Repeals) Bill, The Law Commission and The Scottish Law Commission, presented to Parliament by the Lord Chancellor and Secretary of State

The thirty-eight Acts were related to the construction and maintenance of a railway network in India during British rule from across the seven seas. These laws in strict British interest commanded the workings of the early railway companies. The process of their scrapping was complete by 2013, putting a complete end to that era of Indian Railways.

Most of the Acts enabled companies in the Victorian era to be established and to operate various commercial undertakings in, or in connection with, British India. British India included all territories and places which were governed by the Queen through the Governor General of India.

The repeal proposals were brought in by the Law Commission to review statute law relating to the Indian subcontinent, which remained on the UK statute book after India, Pakistan (and later Bangladesh), Ceylon (subsequently Sri Lanka) and Burma (now Myanmar) achieved independence and sovereign status. While the first phase of the scrapping of Acts tackled the last remaining statutes relating to the former East India Company, the second phase of the project centred on the Indian Railways system. Some thirty-eight railway Acts were repealed by the Statute Law (Repeals) Bill 2013.

Several small and big Acts had been in place since

for Justice before the Scottish Parliament in June 2015. One can read the entire report here: https://s3-eu-west-2.amazonaws.com/lawcom-prod-storage-11jsxou24uy7q/uploads/2015/06/lc357_20th_statute_law_repeals_report.pdf

1853, when the first passenger train in India was run by the Great Indian Peninsula Railway Company, to 1868, when significant British private investment led to the creation of a dozen or more large railway companies (and many smaller), with operations stretching across British India and Ceylon.

Post-1868, the railway network started to develop as a form of state enterprise, either through the government acquiring existing undertakings with the help of the guarantee-surrender mechanism, or by direct investment and construction. Formal transfer of operating assets was secured by a series of Railway Purchase Acts, which provided for the vesting of the relevant undertakings in the Secretary of State, and the termination of various contracts.

Additionally, the legislation would provide for an accumulating sinking fund (to be paid out as capital on the maturing of the fund), with different classes of annuity holder. Nationalization of the railway management did not occur until 1925.

The Indian Railway Annuities (Sinking Funds) Act 1909, related to the investment of sinking fund money for the railway companies, has long been obsolete. In each instance, the railway company was dissolved and the attached sinking fund distributed over the period 1948–1959. By the time of India's and Pakistan's independence in 1947, their railway infrastructure network had been fully nationalized by the government. Each of the Railway Company Purchase Acts (1879–1908) referred to in the

1909 Act has been repealed by the Statute Law (Repeals) Act 2013.[147]

A Few Repealed Acts

- The East Indian Railway Company Purchase Act 1879
- The Eastern Bengal Railway Company Purchase Act 1884
- The Scinde, Punjab and Delhi Railway Purchase Act 1886
- The Great Indian Peninsula Railway Purchase Act 1900
- The Madras Railway Annuities Act 1908

RAIL GAUGE DEBATE BACK TO HAUNT INDIA

When the Delhi Metro Railway was being built, the question of gauge for the line came up and Indian Railways, going by its strong belief in Indian broad gauge, ruled that it had to be that—5 feet 6 inches—and nothing else.

There were differences in opinion. E. Sreedharan, while building the Delhi Metro, had selected standard gauge, 4 ft 8½ in., or simply 1,435 mm, for the simple reason that most of the metro networks around the world used it, providing better speed, safety and manoeuvrability. In fact, not just metro systems, but approximately over 55 per cent of railway lines across the world use this gauge.

---

[147] 'Statute Law Repeals: Twentieth Report Draft Statute Law (Repeals) Bill, The Law Commission and The Scottish Law Commission,' presented to Parliament by the Lord Chancellor and Secretary of State for Justice by Command of Her Majesty, laid before the Scottish Parliament by the Scottish Ministers in June 2015.

Recalling how the debate started, E. Sreedharan explained, 'The Indian Railways, represented by the Chairman of the Railway Board, insisted on broad gauge. Delhi Chief Minister Sheila Dixit wanted standard gauge, but the Ministry of Railways opposed it. Their argument was that the Indian Railways was following the uni-gauge policy. The railways said broad gauge meant more capacity and put forward some arguments. They wanted to thrust broad gauge on us. I proved to them that gauge had nothing to do with capacity. The matter went up to the Cabinet and a meeting was held to discuss the issue. Lal Krishna Advani was the chairman of the committee and other members included the railway minister and the urban development minister. In the first meeting, all were convinced that the Delhi Metro should be standard gauge. But Railway Minister Mamata Banerjee was absent at the meeting. So Advani said it would not be correct to take a final decision in the absence of the Railway Minister against the decision of the Railway Ministry. So we postponed it to another day, when Banerjee would be available. The second meeting, too, was going well and there were discussions about standard gauge. Then, a bombshell was dropped by the Chairman of the Railway Board, V.K. Agrawal. He said if we were going to have standard gauge, the Indian Railways would not be able to certify it because it had no experience with standard gauge. When Agrawal said this, the Urban Development minister Jagmohan was the first to say that if that were the case we would have to go for broad gauge. According to the legal provisions in place, the

Indian Railways is supposed to give safety certification to the Metro Railway. So everybody agreed to go for broad gauge. That is how broad gauge was decided.'[148]

Change of Gauge

Explaining how Maharashtra politician Sharad Pawar played a key role in the change of gauge for Delhi Metro, Sreedharan recalls, 'Fortunately, some time after this meeting, a Group of Ministers was appointed, and Pawar became the chairman of the Group of Ministers. I kept fighting my battle and said, "Delhi Phase I is lost,but why should we continue broad gauge for the rest of the country?" I had a discussion with Pawar. He was fully convinced that standard gauge was best. This was after about a year from the meeting when the decision for broad gauge had been taken. Pawar then volunteered to call another meeting.'

'So, another meeting of the Group of Ministers was called, and it was Pawar who pioneered the decision that the Metro Rail should be standard gauge. Pawar had a vision. He said, "Why should the remaining cities suffer?" He saved the day by putting across a clause that the gauge would be decided with the concurrence of the state governments building the Metro Railway, not by the Indian Railways. Then the Metro Act came in and things changed. The railways [...] continues to create problems, but this decision by Pawar changed everything, and almost all the

---

[148]Personal interaction

state governments went for standard gauge,' he says.[149]

This is the reason the Delhi Metro has two gauges.

A POWER CUT WITH THE PRIME MINISTER ON-BOARD THE INAUGURAL DELHI METRO TRAIN

The first line of the Delhi Metro connecting eastern Delhi's Shahdara to north-central Tis Hazari was ready by 2002. Trials were flagged off by the then Deputy Prime Minister Lal Krishna Advani in September 2002, and Prime Minister Atal Bihari Vajpayee threw it open for the public a day before Christmas, on 24 December 2002.

The response was immense, with citizens of Delhi eager to take a ride, and overcrowding causing the ticketing system to collapse. But a lesser-known incident was of a power cut on the Metro network when the Prime Minister and his team were on-board the train. But due to the Delhi Metro Rail Corporation's (DMRC) foresight, the power cut was never noticed!

How Delhi Metro Overcame Murphy's Law

On 24 December 2002, when the Prime Minister of India was to open the first section, DMRC had only one substation at Kashmere Gate feeding 220 kV. While highly unlikely, there was still an apparent risk of system failure.

---

[149]Personal interview with Dr E. Sreedharan. Also, *India's Railway Man—A Biography of Dr E. Sreedharan* by Rajendra B. Aklekar, Rupa Publications, 2017

Many other organizations might have overlooked such a risk, but DMRC was committed to displaying its quality and insisted on a backup, but there was no alternative available. However, the concerned DMRC official noticed that the Northern Railways have an independent supply at Dadri and a substation at Sahibabad. DMRC requested them for help and laid one line till Shahdara (25 kV) as a backup arrangement, at an extra cost.

On 24 December, the PM was the first citizen to take a ride on the Metro. The journey started at 10.10 a.m. and then, at 10.20, the power supply was disrupted. Within a minute the backup system took over without anyone even noticing the failure of the primary system.

On the day of the inauguration of the Metro, with the who's who of Indian politics on board, and with the media watching, falling prey to Murphy's Law was averted, since careful preparation and commitment had been put in place to go the extra mile, and the embarrassment was avoided.

—Satish Kumar, Director (Electrical)/DMRC during an interaction with students of the Indian Institute of Management, Ahmedabad.[150]

---

[150] Anuj Dayal, 'Professional Competency,' *25 Management Strategies for Delhi Metro Success—The Sreedharan Way*, (Chief PRO, DMRC, April 2012) p.41

SHAKUNTALA RAILWAY—TRAVELLING BACK IN TIME

The Shakuntala Express remains a symbol of romanticism. It has nothing to do with Kalidasa and his Sanskrit work *Abhijñāna Shākuntalam*, but is a vestige of the British Raj era. The line is one of the last pieces of the colonial railway legacy that was never nationalized. The result—the railways still pays the Central Provinces Railway company that technically owns the line.

The story goes that a British firm, Killick, Nixon and Company, set up in 1857, created the Central Provinces Railway Company (CPRC) to act as its agents. The company built a 2 foot 6 inch (762 mm) narrow gauge line in 1910 to carry cotton from the interior areas of Vidarbha to the Murtajapur junction on the main broad gauge line to Mumbai, from where it would be shipped to Manchester in England.[151] Murtajapur junction was the focal point of this railway, and the train was popularly known as 'Vidarbha Queen'.

Murtajapur/Murtijapur is in Maharashtra (Akola district) and is a junction in Bhusawal division of Central Railway (CR), along the main Mumbai-Nagpur-Howrah broad gauge line. However, a narrow gauge line also passes through Murtazapur, divided into a 76–km

---

[151] 'Shakuntala Railways: India's only private railway line,' *The Economic Times,* Dec 11, 2016, https://economictimes.indiatimes.com/slideshows/infrastructure/shakuntala-railways-indias-only-private-railway-line/colonial-relic/slideshow/55924730.cms

northern stretch between Murtazapur and Achalpur/ Ellichpur and a 113–km south-eastern stretch between Murtazapur and Yeotmal/Yavatmal.

The Yavatmal stretch was opened in 1903 and Achalpur stretch in 1913. Both segments were constructed and operated by the Great Indian Peninsula Railway (GIPR). In 1925, GIPR became a part of the Indian Railways. Therefore, as a legacy, the Indian Railways started to operate narrow gauge trains along the Shakuntala Railway (the train is known as Shakuntala Express).

Locomotives were initially steam ones, replaced with diesel in 1995. The ageing old infrastructure is still in use and evokes a sense of nostalgia.

Shakuntala Railway is still owned by CPRC, presumably because the government of the day simply forgot to nationalize it. The CPRC and Killick Nixon have moved from British to Indian hands.

There is a contract between CPRC and the Central Railway (CR) under which the CPRC can keep 55 per cent of passenger revenue, giving the rest to CR. Naturally, CPRC is meant to maintain rail tracks. But it doesn't possess the resources and the CR has refused to pay it, since they have been spending on its maintenance. The result is a judicial dispute.[152]

Interestingly, the CRPC is now based in Borivali, Mumbai, and the company's 107th Annual Report

---

[152] 'Shakuntala's woes,' *Business Standard*, September 13, 2015, http://www.business-standard.com/article/opinion/bibek-debroy-shakuntala-s-woes-115091300746_1.html

states that the Central Railway had demanded a sum of ₹18.72 crore in December 2002 towards repairs, rehabilitation, renewals and replacements of the railway assets.

The Indian Railways have, meanwhile, listed the line to be converted into a main line broad gauge and the line, as it existed, is set to become history for ever.

THE SECOND COMING

Do trains have life? If they do, the one I am going to talk about has had its rebirth. And that too, a glorious one. One Electric Multiple Unit (EMU) railway coach has shown how invincible the Indian Railways are in letter and spirit.

864-A is an old trailer rail coach with rundown looks comprising first- and second-class compartments. But don't go by its looks; it's just due to its age and overuse. It has a strong backbone and a stronger heart and is fit and sturdy enough to ferry Mumbai's 'super-dense crush load', a term coined by the railways to describe extreme crowding on the city's suburban railway network.

It now runs on what is the Trans-Harbour section of the Mumbai railway, connecting the two cities of Thane and Navi Mumbai. Most of the EMU local trains on Mumbai's suburban network have been upgraded with the new Siemens class or Bombardier class trains under a World Bank-funded project. They are well ventilated, have sleek looks and provide a good riding experience. But a few old ones are yet to complete their service life. This particular old-fashioned class of train I am talking about is hated by the present generation of commuters for being 'stuffy, resembling a cage' and is often called a khatara (scrap). It, however, remains a feast for rail fans for it being 'art deco', a vanishing relic of the old DC electric era and having served an entire generation. Originally made by Jessop Kolkata, these class of trains have unique, rectangular symmetrical features as compared to the trains manufactured by the Integral Coach Factory in Chennai, which have become a more common feature now. This one is one of them. But wait to read about the exceptional story of this khatara 'cage' that has made its mark like none other!

◆

Let me take you back to the horrific day of 11 July 2006, a Tuesday. Covering the transport beat for *Hindustan Times*, Mumbai, I was at my desk when my editor, Samar Halarnkar, walked up to me and mentioned that there had been some kind of chaos on the railway lines, a fire or an explosion. I dialled my sources and officials frantically, but there was no clarity in what they said. My first instinct was to run to the nearest railway station to know what exactly had happened. Our office was then at Mahim, close to the railway station, and as I was about to reach there I could see a sea of people rushing away from the train station, some ambulances and police vehicles. I walked towards the station. I gathered that there had been a series of bombings on the trains. As I reached the station, there was pandemonium, with mutilated bodies being brought from the rail lines and bleeding, injured people being put into cabs and carts to be taken to hospital. It was raining too, and the smell of burnt flesh and metal was all over the place. Light fumes of smoke could still be seen from the rain-cooled metal of the burnt train coach. The first class train compartment had been ripped apart and bodies and limbs were strewn around. My heart beat faster than ever as I saw locals trying to help the injured amidst cries of help. The train stood dead silent with the overhead wires snapped and lying on top of it. As I walked up the Mahim platform, I saw that a section of the roof on Platform 3 had a big hole in it, the point where the blast had occurred. Body parts of people were lying all over the rail tracks.

Walking a few minutes from there in the traffic, I reached Matunga, where there was another disfigured train coach, ripped open due to the impact of the bomb, and the same smell of flesh and metal, mixed with pouring rain. The mobile networks were all jammed. All I remember from the glimpses from Matunga overbridge was the mutilated coach No. 864-A. That evening, there had been seven blasts in seven trains in about 11 minutes, killing over 200 passengers in an abominable act of terrorism.

The sights at the Mahim and Matunga stations with bodies and mangled train coaches are etched in my memory for life. Even till six months later, I could identify the spot of the blast at Mahim station, as a tubelight was still missing from the station. The burnt 864-A coach at Matunga, too, lived on in my memory.

◆

August 2018. Twelve years down the line. I am travelling in coach 864-A. Yes. The same coach that I had seen at Matunga station. Of the seven blast-affected rail coaches, five had been restored within one year at a cost of ₹1–1.2 crore but were slowly phased out in these years. Two coaches had been immediately 'condemned', as they were beyond repair. I had been following them, writing about them for the next few years, but later forgot about them. But earlier that month, when I heard that 864-A, the only one among the restored, had lived on and had been shifted to a different passenger line, I could not hold myself back.

I waited for it for three hours, and there it was! They had not changed the number, and this coach was part of a twelve-car train on the Thane-Vashi section. I climbed the same first class coach for travel. I stood transfixed. The photographic images of that horrific day in my memory, the burning smell of metal and flesh in the air and incessant rains of that July evening came rushing back to me. As the train moved out of the station, swerving across the country's oldest rail bridge over the Thane creek, and caught pace, I felt a sense of pride and patriotism on how this one rail coach had been a slap in the face of terrorism. It had lived on, defeating the purpose of terrorism. I travelled in it for the next two rides, Up and Down, filled with emotion, nostalgia and honour. 864-A lives on and so does the country's resilience. My salute to the Indian Railways!

◆

864-A, the damaged coach of the twelve–car 5.57-p.m. Churchgate-Virar local that was torn apart at Matunga Road station had been made by Jessop & Company, Kolkata and all the material required for restoration, including the frames of the outer shell and the rods supporting it, had been bought from the original company.

In most of the coaches subjected to the attack, the roof had been severely damaged. The main frame of the coach, the backbone of the structure, had sagged and needed replacement. The damaged roof structure had been replaced with metal sheets from original spares. After restoring the main frame, accessories like seats, fans and other such items had been installed. Finally, bogie frames with wheels were attached. After all this was done, various checks like oscillation tests and trial runs under various conditions had been conducted; there were empty runs as well as trials, with loads varying from 20–30 tons, making it fit for a second innings. In 2006, after it was restored, along with four other coaches, it underwent extensive tests before it was declared fit to run. A run of these carriages was also simulated in the workshop under the most difficult conditions and only when the authorities cleared all the set parameters were these coaches put back into service.

After restoration of the coach, it had been transferred to Central Railway as part of an exchange programme while upgrading Mumbai Railway's electric network from the old DC to alternating current (AC). 864–A and a few other older DC coaches were part of this exchange.

The coach was retired in September 2018. And the

Central Railway promised to preserve this one's dignity at a rail museum, so that its story could be told to future generations. The story of its rebirth is a story that every Indian should be proud of.

STORIES AROUND INDIA'S FIRST BULLET TRAIN

As India is now gearing up for the next generation of trains in the form of the bullet train, things are coming full circle. Originally proposed by Prime Minister Manmohan Singh hoping to develop world class passenger systems, high speed passenger trains running at 350 kmph were first mentioned in the Parliament by Railway Minister Lalu Prasad Yadav in February 2007.

He said, 'India is today seen as a growing power in the world. The rapid growth of the economy, rising industrialization and urbanization, and unprecedented growth in intercity travel have opened up infinite possibilities for developing high speed passenger corridors. Therefore, we have decided to conduct pre-feasibility studies for construction of high speed passenger corridors, equipped with state-of-the-art signalling and train control systems, for running high speed trains at 300–350 kmph; one each in the northern, western, southern and eastern regions of the country.'[153]

The idea moved ahead in his February 2009 Interim Budget speech, where he announced among five different

---

[153]Speech of Railway Minister Shri Lalu Prasad Yadav, introducing the Railway Budget 2007–2008, February 26, 2007, Point no.40

corridors, the Ahmedabad-Mumbai-Pune route with work 'soon to begin for a pre-feasibility study'. The proposed stations, including Lonavala in the Mumbai–Pune section and Surat, Bharuch and Vadodara in the Mumbai-Ahmedabad section, would have an eventual extension to Bengaluru.

Agreements followed in 2013 with the French National Railways, Société Nationale des Chemins de Fer Français (SNCF), for technical cooperation and feasibility report for 'operations and development'. The Pune section was dropped due to the mountainous ghat terrain that could lead to cost escalation, leaving just the Mumbai-Ahmedabad corridor as feasible.

The Japanese Come In

In September the same year, India signed a deal for a joint feasibility study[154] with Japanese Prime Minister Shinzo Abe during his India visit in December 2015, offering an attractive ₹79,000-crore loan for a period of fifty years with a moratorium of fifteen years, at an interest rate of 0.1 per cent. The project was on with a body called the National High Speed Rail Corporation Limited (NHSRCL) in place by January 2016 and Prime Minister Abe back in India to lay the foundation stone

---

[154]'Joint statement on Indian Prime Minister's visit to Japan: Strengthening the strategic and global partnership between India and Japan beyond the 60th anniversary of diplomatic relations,' Press Information Bureau, Government of India, Prime Minister's Office, May 29, 2013, Point no.15

for the project, along with Prime Minister Narendra Modi, in September 2017.

By September 2018, much of the preparatory work was on full swing. There was a training centre, and a bridge span longer than the one on the Japanese network (220 m) coming up over Vadodara station.[155] But as the project gathers momentum, voices have begun to be raised over land acquisition issues by farmers, land owners and villagers. There have been protests, petitions in courts and appeals to the Japanese to put the project on hold.

Rumours Bring in a Sense of Déjà Vu

There is a sense of déjà vu here. Naysayers and members of the Opposition have fuelled rumours along the stretches of villages, somewhat similar to the time when the first trains were introduced. Here are a few of the objections stated.[156]

- With the bullet train whizzing past over our farms, there will be radiation and vibrations of all kinds and it will affect agriculture and farms, turning the land barren.
- People who are stakeholders for the bullet train are looking for land, and for it to come up, entire villages will be relocated to interior districts of Maharashtra, like Satara or Sangli.

---

[155]Site visits by author

[156]Compiled from personal interaction with villagers along the proposed corridor, Dahanu Town Mayor Bharat Rajput and from notes of Chief Public Relations Officer, National High Speed Rail Corporation Limited, Dhananjay Kumar.

- Due to side filling of tracks of bullet trains, the fertile land will be converted into wetlands.
- This is just a ploy to displace all the tribal population around Palghar district of Thane to make way for future projects like the Mumbai-Delhi industrial corridor.
- After a few years of laying tracks, the stakeholders will come again to acquire more land.

A few villagers even came up with absurd demands saying they now intended to plan start-ups, but now, with land being utilized for the bullet train project, they want the share of twenty years' profit of the proposed business deal.

The project now seems to be moving ahead, and as of March 2019, the NHSRCL has called in tenders for design, construction, testing and commissioning of a 237-km-long main line for the Mumbai–Ahmedabad High Speed Rail corridor. This is about 47 per cent of the total alignment of 508 km. The work will be undertaken between Zaroli village at the Maharashtra–Gujarat border and Vadodara in Gurjarat, elevated except for one mountain tunnel of about 280 m. There will be twenty-four river crossings and thirty road and canal crossings. The entire alignment will have four stations—Vapi, Bilimora, Surat and Bharuch (all in Gujarat). About 30 per cent of the land required for the project has been acquired, and NHSRCL expects that by the time the tender will be finalized in November 2019, the required land will be available. The corridor of Mumbai-Ahmedabad has been proposed with twelve stations in mind, i.e., Mumbai, Thane, Virar, Boisar, Vapi, Bilimora, Surat, Bharuch, Vadodara, Anand/Nadia, Ahmedabad and Sabarmati, all near major traffic points. Two depots have been proposed on either ends of the corridor—one near Thane and the other near Sabarmati rail depot.

TRAIN 18: VANDE BHARAT EXPRESS—INDIA'S 18-MONTH MARVEL

In 2018, Indian Railways created an iconic semi-high-speed train set code-named Train 18, publicly named the Vande Bharat Express. The sixteen-coach Train 18 designed for a speed of 160 kmph was conceived, designed and developed in a record of time of about 18 months, as against the industry demand of about three-four years by the ICF Chennai at an approximate cost of ₹100 crore, half the price of importing such a train. The train has about 80 per cent Indian origin components.[157]

Sudhanshu Mani, the determined general manager of ICF (now retired), who took over in 2016, said,

> I decided that we must build a modern train set as it would be now or never, at least for me. I learnt that the project had been turned down, primarily because it did not find support of some departments. But I met Railway Board Chairman A.K. Mittal, who

---

[157]Integral Coach Factory, https://icf.indianrailways.gov.in/view_section. jsp?lang=0&id=0,294

agreed and overruled everyone to grant us the sanction within days. We sat down for multiple meetings circa March/April and finalized the concept. And to make sure that the project did not hit any roadblock with change of leadership, we were going to do it well before I retire, that is, before December 2018. The prototype train must be out of ICF in 2018 itself, and so we called it Train 18. It was sheer hard work from there on.

Our meetings with foreign consultants were always very interesting. A typical meeting would go on without a break from 9 a.m. to 8 p.m., which they were not so accustomed to. The Chief Design Engineer (Mechanical) S. Srinivas always ordered pizzas for lunch in the middle of technical discussions. Occasionally, a consultant would fall sick, perhaps due to overwork, but we conveniently blamed it on the change in content and pattern of meals. Invariably, those falling sick would come back cured for the meetings within a day or two; we had managed to Indianize them. Once, at one of the concluding sessions, I asked if the visitors had gone around Chennai and nearby places of interest. The poor chaps replied that for that to happen, I had to advise the CDE/M to loosen a bit and go easy. In one of the meetings, an ICF designer asked a Polish consultant during the makeshift lunch, 'Why don't you bring your girlfriend along next time to Chennai?' The Polish gentleman quipped, 'What! In this madness with you guys! You want her to leave me for good, or what.'[158]

There are many such anecdotes, most of them being of sheer hard work and determination. Train 18 was ready by October 2018 with the Prime Minister acknowledging the effort by saying, 'In the last four and a half years, we have tried to transform the condition of the Indian Railways sincerely and with a lot of hard work. Vande Bharat Express is a glimpse of that effort.'[159]

[158]Sudhanshu Mani, 'Memoirs,' http://anindecisiveindian.blogspot.com/?view=flipcard

[159]English rendering of PM's speech at the flagging off function of Vande Bharat Express, Press Information Bureau, February 15, 2019, http://www.pib.nic.in/PressReleseDetail.aspx?PMO=3&PRID=1564704

Conclusion

What I have presented in this book are just nuggets and anecdotes and not a comprehensive history of the nearly two-hundred-year journey of the Indian Railways, yet I am hoping it has given one a sense of the genesis, magnitude and the spread of the iron web in India.

Every Indian has probably undertaken a rail journey some time in his life and cannot forget the reverberating sounds of 'Chai, chai', the large window bars and the monotonous announcements at stations and the exhaustion and excitement of undertaking a train journey. The Railways have been an inseparable part of Indian journeys since its inception. The people stories, the social changes they brought about and the way the transporter has effectively touched every sphere of life right from the time the British ruled India to the days of our freedom struggle and from the days of India becoming a republic to today's growth years, would all, individually, make different odysseys.

This book is a sincere effort to capture the flavours of those journeys through through anecdotes, tales and documented incidents, chosen randomly but with attributions and endorsements, wherever possible. And that is the reason the book has so many quotes, to maintain originality through a narrative. There might be some incident or development which may not have been captured in its entirety, since the book shares nuggets of information without prejudice. A few authenticated anecdotes may even be thought to be disputed but have been included for the readers' pleasure, to maintain the flow after basic corroboration.

The aim is to chronologically weave the nuggets to give a sense of history, geography and even sociology of India and shows how deeply the railways are embedded in the Indian psyche.

With the recent developments in the sector, it is now the age of metro trains and high speed rail. Indian Railways seems to have come full circle from Arthur Cotton's experiments on the Red Hill Railway near Chennai to the manufacture of the hi-tech, hi-speed Train 18, the Vande Bharat Express, by Sudhanshu Mani and his team, again, near Chennai. I must say the journey of Indian Railways has now indeed picked up pace. Godspeed!

Acknowledgements

This work would not have been possible without those rattling trains of the Indian Railways that run day and night, inspiring and charging me up. My first thanks to Ajai Banerjee, the passionate railway and aviation veteran, who was kind enough to go through the draft, suggest changes, corrections and authenticate details. I am indebted to him as I could fall back on him for the smallest of queries at any point of time. While Sir Mark Tully's words of encouragment and tips have brought a new vigour to the book, Bibek Debroy's works proved to be a rudder, providing direction and movement to the flow of the writing, and I am thankful to both of them for the same. Besides being always grateful to my inspiration, Dr E. Sreedharan sir, I also have to thank retired railwayman Ashutosh K. Banerji, now in his 80s—one of the key members of the Rajdhani Express launch team—who was kind enough to get back with whatever details he could remember of the iconic train launch. Also, a big thanks to Shekhar Krishnan who went through the Railway Time chapter. Mention is also required of the former managing director of Konkan Railway and inventor, B. Rajaram, for authenticating the details of excerpts on how the Konkan Railway offices were initially set up, and Achal Khare, the managing director of India's National High Speed Rail Corporation, the ambitious bullet train project, for a hearty chat about various aspects of the ambitious rail corridor and the creator and retired General Manager of Integral Coach Factory, Sudhanshu Mani. Not to leave out Mumbai's heritage evangelist Khaki Tours' Bharat Gothoskar and National Rail Museum Delhi's Subhabrata Chattopadhyay. I also thank my editors at Mid-Day, Tinaz Nooshian and Sanjeev Shivadekar, for allowing me to pursue this book with unwavering passion.

All this, of course, would not have been possible without my family, wife Priya and sister Pradnya, who never complained about my mental absence during such projects, and my daughters, Tanvi and Vaibhavi, who came up with ideas to add spice to the work.

Index

A.H. Wheeler & Co., 135
Abe, Shinzo, 203. *See also* Bullet train
Acworth, Sir William Mitchell, 108
Adam, Hargrave Lee, 127
Advani, Lal Krishna, 191, 193
Agrawal, V.K., 191
Agri Horticultural Society, 8
Akhbar Anjuman, 78
Allied forces, Operational command
  of, 141
Along Lost Lines, 137
Ambulances and Tanks, 147–48
Anderson, G.A., 93
Anglo-Afghan War, 81–82
Annai Indira Gandhi Bridge, 173
Assam Bengal Railway (ABR), 117,
  142
Atterbury, Paul, 137
Azad Hind Fauj, 157–59
Azad, Chandrasekhar, 156

Baba Bhalku Rail Museum, 99
Bakshi, Sachindra, 156
Ballard, J.E., 131, 138–39
Banaji, Seth Framji Cowasji, 7
Banerjee, Mamata, 191
Banerji, Ashutosh K., 173–76
Bankura Damodar Railway (BDR),
  125
Baroda Railway, 90–92
Bhalku, Baba, 98–99
Big-rail-small-rail debate, 86–90

arguments for small trains, 88–90
arguments against, 86–88
Bisht, B.M.S., 157
Bismil, Ram Prasad, 156–57
bizarre stories, 51–53
Boat trains, 137–40
  Bombay to Karachi, 137–38
  Bombay to Peshawar, 139–40
  Frontier Mail, 139–40
Bombay, 42–45
  clash of cultures, 42
  invincible prejudices, 42–43
  odds and unpredictable hurdles,
    44–45
  rigid work practices, 43
  strike, 42
  superstition, 42
Bombay Presidency, 110, 115
Bombay Quarterly Review, 43
Bombay Telegraph, 48
Bombay, Baroda and Central India
  Railway (BB&CI Railway),
  90–92, 104, 110–11, 139, 162,
  167
Bombay-Thana railway line, 3, 54
Bose, Subhash Chandra, 157. *See also*
  Azad Hind Fauj
Boyd Sinclair, 142
'Branded' boat trains, 138
Bruce, George, 60–63
Brunton, John, 56–58
Building the Railways of the Raj, 42

Bullet train, 202–6
agreements with French National
Railways, 203
deal with Japan, 203–4
Bullock carts, 27, 54–56

Calcutta Chronicle, 38
Carey, William, 8
Carroll, E.B., 92
Cautley, Sir Proby T., 21–22
Central Provinces Railway Company
(CPRC), 195–97
Chakravarty, Keshab, 156
Challenges, xii, 32–33, 90, 93, 98
Chandra, Goluk, 6, 8
China Burma India (CBI) theatre,
141–42
Choudhury, A.B.A. Ghani Khan,
179–80
'Climate peculiarities and
circumstances', 32
Consolidation process, 110
Cotton, 27–28, 50, 55, 195
Cotton, Arthur Tomas, 9, 11–12, 16,
18–20, 210
development of a 'rotatory' engine, 19
Covell, W.E.R., 143
Creek, Vasai, 111
Cyclone, 169–73

Dalhousie, Lord, 29, 53, 72, 84
Darjeeling Himalayan Railway, 94–96
Debroy, Bibek, 110
Defence mechanisms and protection
measures, 77
Defence Unit, 147
Déjà vu, 204–5
Delhi Metro Rail, 190–94
change of gauge, 192–93
Murphy's Law, 193–94
Desai, Kishore, 110
Difficulties in building railways, 33–34
Dismissals and transfers, 181
Dixit, Sheila, 191
Double murder on the GIP Railway,
130–34

East Bengal Railway, 104
East India Company, 31–32, 52–53,
59, 71, 101, 188
East India Iron Company, 20
East Indian Railway, 31, 36–37, 52–53,
66–67, 72–73, 81, 121, 146, 190
East India Railway Committee, 108
East Indian Railway Magazine, 146
Eastern Bengal Railway, 95, 104, 190
Egmore, 2–3, 5
Electric Multiple Units (EMUs), 3,
113
Electric Railways, 110–13
Elephants buying, 66–67
Employers' and Workmen' (Disputes)
Act (X), 44
English Channel to the Indus rail,
52–53
Experimental Line
Bombay to Thane, 31
Calcutta to Rajmahal, 31
'Extreme Railway' on Bikes, 182–84
Ezhumbur, 3

Falkland, Lord Viscount, 47
Fare cut, 185–86. *See also* Yadav, Lalu
Prasad
Faviell and Fowler, 47
Faviell, William Fredrick, 42
Fernandes, George, 183
'Fire Chariot', 48
First class carriages, 60–62
First rails, 22–23
First Rajdhani, secrets of, 173–76
critics, 173
feasibility of increasing speeds, 176
new technology, 173
objections, 174–75
responses, 175–76
First steam engine, 8
First train, 1, 6, 16–18, 37, 60, 81,
187, 204
engine with two people on an
incline, 17–18
four-car train, 16

two-car train, 17
First War of Independence, 71. *See also* Mutiny of 1857
Forde, A.W., 91
Fowler, Henry, 42–43
Fowler, John, 88
Franco-Prussian War, 87
Frankfurt, Treaty of, 87
Freedom from wheelbarrows and baskets, 24
Frere, Sir Henry Bartle Edward, 57–58
Friend of India, 40
Frontier Mail, 139–40

Gaekwar dynasty, 90
Gaekwar's Baroda State Railway (GBSR), 90
Gandhi, Indira, 179
Gandhi, Mahatma, 150, 159–61
    Asthi special train, 161
    conspiracy to assassinate, 159
    journeys in third class coaches, 150–54
    third class coach for funeral, 161
Ganges Canal Works, 21
Ganguli, Bankim Chandra, 177
Golden Temple Mail, 139. *See also* Frontier Mail
Gracias, Carmo, 183
Great Indian Peninsula Railway (GIPR), 28–29, 31, 36, 47, 55, 67–69, 104, 110–11, 130–31, 138–39, 166, 187, 189–90, 196
Greenwich Mean Time (GMT), 115–16
Greenwich Meridian, 115
Grenades and armoured cars, 146–48
Gujral, Mohinder Singh, 179–80
Gun Carriage Factory, 7
Gupt, Mammathnath, 156

Halarnkar, Samar, 198
Halt Station India: The Dramatic Tale of the Nation's First Lines, 6
Hanumanthaiya, Kengal , 178

Harijan, 160
Harris, Lord, 1
Haunted Rail Tunnel, 97–100
    Barog tunnel, 98
    haunting tales, 99
    tunnel at Solan Brewery, 97
Mr Hawkshaw, 87
Head-on collision of official and minister, 179–81
Herilngton, H.S., 98
High Speed Rail, 187, 205, 210
Hindustan Republican Association (HRA), 155–56
HMS Dekagree, 37
HMS Goodwin, 37
Hodgson, John, 37–38
House of Commons, 27, 86, 89
Howrah, 21, 30, 36–41, 51, 136, 146, 167, 176, 195
    landlord holds up the works, 40
    'no compensation', 38
    woman in childbirth, 39
The Hurkaru, 39–40

The Illustrated London News, 73
Imperial War Museums, 107
Improving efficiency, 143–45
Improvization experiments, 18–20
India-Burma (IBT) theatres, 141
Indian Broad Gauge, 85, 190
Indian National Army (INA), 157. *Also see* Azad Hind Fauj
Indian Penal Code, 156
Indian Railway Annuities (Sinking Funds) Act, 189
Indian Railway Library, 135
Indian Railway Traffic Service (IRTS), 157, 179
Indian Railways Fans' Club Association, 60, 124, 138, 146, 159
Indian Steel and Iron Company, 20. *Also see* Porto Novo Iron Works
Informal Operations, 143
Integral Coach Factory (ICF), 175, 198, 206–7, 212

Internal finances of the railways, 108
International gauge, 84
International Meridian Conference, 115

Jackson, Ernest, 139
Jagmohan, 191
Jamalpur Loco Workshop, 81
James Andrew Broun-Ramsay, 29
Jeep locos, 141–45
Jessop & Company, 201
Jules Verne classic, inspiration from, 67–70
Jungle Life of India, 64

Kakori train dacoity, 150, 154–57
Kalka–Simla Railway (KSR), 95, 97–99
Kerr, Ian J., 42–43, 124
Key directive, 30
Khan, Ashfaqulla, 156–57
Khan, Shah Nawaz, 157
Kipling's Rail Romance, 135–37
Konkan Railway, xii, 182–83, 212

Lahiri, Rajendra, 156
Laird, Cammell, 113
Lal, B.B., 180
Lal, Banwari, 156
Lal, Mukundi, 156
Locomotive, 23–24
    death of, 25
'Lokhandi rakshas', 49
London Underground, 111
Loop line in railway parlance, 96

MacArthur's War Design (MAWD), 148–49. *See also* War locomotives
'Made in Porto Novo', 4. *See also* Porto Novo
Madras Corps of Engineers, 9, 20
Madras Herald, 10
Madras Railway Company, 59
Madras railway network, 60
Mahananda Wildlife Sanctuary, 94
'Make in India', 6

Malshej Ghats, alignment through, 28
Manchester Commercial Association, 28
Mani, Sudhanshu, 206, 208, 210
Markings and the type of rails, 2
Marshall, Josiah, 4
Matheran Hill Railway, 92–93
Maude, Frederick Stanley, 106
Mayo, Lord, 85, 87
'Mechanical agents', 9
Memon merchant, 152
Merz, C.H., 111
Messrs Stewart and Company, 37
Metro Act, 192
Metros, 187
Metz of India, 87
Military considerations, 72
Military Railway Service, 143
'Milkman' rail minister, 185–86. *See also* Yadav, Lalu Prasad
Minister of Railways' Award, 173. *See also* Sreedharan, E.
Mishaps, 37
Mittal, A.K., 206
Modi, Narendra, 203
Monday afternoon massacre, 179–81
Moreau, Émile, 135
Morning Chronicle, 41
Mughal-style architecture, 4
Mumbai train bomb blasts (2006), xii, 198–99
Murphy's Law, 193–94
Mutiny of 1857, 56–57, 71–73, 77, 80
My Memories of INA and its Netaji, 157

Nagalingam, K., 172
Naiyyar, Pyare Lal, 161
Narayan, Prabhavati, 161
Narrow Gauge Train, Battles of, 95–97
National High Speed Rail Corporation Limited (NHSRCL), 203, 205
National Rail Museum, 100–1, 112, 122
Nayyar, Sushila, 161